When Life Gives You Lemons

When life gives you lemons

Turning *sour* photos into *sweet* scrapbook layouts

Sherry Steveson

MEMORY MAKERS BOOKS

Cincinnati, Ohio
www.mycraftivity.com

About the Author

▶ **Sherry Steveson** has been passionate about scrapbooking for more than 10 years. Finding a hobby that merged her love for photography with her gift of writing, all wrapped up in a creative outlet, was the catalyst for a lifelong devotion. Her work has been published in many of the major scrapbook magazines and idea books, and it always brings a thrill to her family when they see their faces in the pages of those publications. She's also found her calling in the world of teaching scrapbooking to others. Sherry currently maintains a blog at www.sherrysteveson.typepad.com/my_weblog. When she isn't writing, scrapbooking or teaching, she maintains a very full schedule with her three children and her husband's landscape business.

12 11 10 09 08   5 4 3 2 1

Distributed in Canada by Fraser Direct
100 Armstrong Avenue
Georgetown, ON, Canada L7G 5S4
Tel: (905) 877-4411

Distributed in the U.K. and Europe by David & Charles
Brunel House, Newton Abbot, Devon, TQ12 4PU, England
Tel: (+44) 1626 323200, Fax: (+44) 1626 323319
E-mail: postmaster@davidandcharles.co.uk

Distributed in Australia by Capricorn Link
P.O. Box 704, S. Windsor, NSW 2756 Australia
Tel: (02) 4577-3555

Library of Congress Cataloging-in-Publication Data

Steveson, Sherry.
  When life gives you lemons / Sherry Steveson. -- 1st ed.
    p. cm.
  Includes bibliographical references and index.
  ISBN 978-1-59963-024-3 (softcover : alk. paper)
  1. Photograph albums. 2. Scrapbooks. I. Title.
  TR501.S74 2008
  745.593--dc22

                    2008014050

fw

F+W PUBLICATIONS, INC.
www.fwpublications.com

Metric Conversion Chart

to convert	to	multiply by
Inches	Centimeters	2.54
Centimeters	Inches	0.4
Feet	Centimeters	30.5
Centimeters	Feet	0.03
Yards	Meters	0.9
Meters	Yards	1.1
Sq. Inches	Sq. Centimeters	6.45
Sq. Centimeters	Sq. Inches	0.16
Sq. Feet	Sq. Meters	0.09
Sq. Meters	Sq. Feet	10.8
Sq. Yards	Sq. Meters	0.8
Sq. Meters	Sq. Yards	1.2
Pounds	Kilograms	0.45
Kilograms	Pounds	2.2
Ounces	Grams	28.3
Grams	Ounces	0.035

Editor *Kristin Boys*
Designer *Kelly O'Dell*
Art Coordinator *Eileen Aber*
Production Coordinator *Greg Nock*
Photographer *Ric Deliantoni*
Stylist *Jan Nickum*

dedication

I would like to dedicate this book to my husband, Jason, without whom I would not be able to pursue my passions. He provides the love and support I need to follow my dreams. To my three children, Jacob, Madison and Fletcher, who are an extension of my own heart and make the journey of life worthwhile. To my parents, for guiding me and encouraging me in all I do. To my sister, Nicole, who never doubted me for a second. To Kimber and Janet, who are my confidants and best friends, and without whom this book would not be possible.

acknowledgments

I couldn't have done this without the confidence that Christine Doyle, Kristin Boys and Eileen Aber placed in me. Your unbelievable guidance and encouragement helped me tremendously during my first foray into authorship.

I appreciate the hard work and talent of my contributors: Kimber McGray, Janet Ohlson, Nic Howard, Suzy Plantamura, Hillary Heidelberg, Kelly Noel and Linda Harrison.

To the wonderful friends and family who have offered their lemons in the hopes that I would turn them into sweet pages: Your confidence in me made the project an enjoyable experience.

big bubbles!

A super cheap Target find ... just one dollar for BIG bubbles and tons of outside fun!

Turning Sour Photos into Sweet Scrapbook Layouts

Through the years, I've taken rolls of film to the photo developer with expectations of spectacular results. Imagine my surprise and disappointment when I discovered that those "once in a lifetime" photos didn't meet my expectations!

As hard as we try to get the perfect photo, sometimes things go wrong. Digital cameras may have made it easier to discover a photo flaw instantly, but they don't allow you to relive moments. We all have those photos we want to do over. Unfortunately, the time machine has yet to be developed, so we are forced to work with less-than-perfect photos of our memories.

I used to tuck bad photos away instead of using them in my scrapbooks. I found it difficult to get inspired by a sour photo. Plus, the best photos are often what get featured on pages in scrapbook magazines, leaving us with few examples of how to work with flawed photos.

Over time, I have learned some tricks for making great scrapbook pages using flawed photos. I'll share with you those recipes for making lemonade on your layouts. I hope you'll discover the possibilities in your own photos and that they'll inspire you to turn your lemons into sweet scrapbook pages.

What Makes a Photo Sour?

Regardless of your skills as a photographer, you're going to end up with at least a few photos that are of less-than-stellar quality. Common photo flaws—like poor lighting and blur—can be hard to avoid no matter how hard you try. But they say that beauty is in the eye of the beholder—and I agree. Just because a photo has some flaws doesn't mean it can't tell a sweet story. Here, find out what the common photo flaws are and how they happen. Then read on to find out how to make them into layout lemonade.

Photo Flaw
Blur

This photo *faux pas* often happens as we are in a hurry to capture a spontaneous moment. Action-filled events, such as sports or holiday celebrations, create the perfect environment for blur. Active children who refuse to cooperate with the photographer can make it difficult to achieve a blur-free photo. Other factors, like low light and a shaky camera, can also contribute to blurred images.

➤ *Can you really incorporate blur into a great layout? Find out on pages 64-67.*

Photo Flaw
Clashing Colors

Photos with colors that clash or are difficult to match aren't necessarily bad in and of themselves. But they can become a problem when you try scrapbooking them and find it difficult to choose a suitable color scheme for a page. Sometimes it's nearly impossible to coordinate the colors in a group of people.

➤ *No, you can't color coordinate your whole life, but you can work with colors in any photo. Flip to page 56 for the hue how-to.*

Photo Flaw

Grain and Other Noise

Pixilated or grainy photos often occur when the shutter speed is set too high. Older film quality, like that in this photo, can also contribute to a grainy image.

> ➤ *Don't groan about grain and other noise. Page 50 reveals how to deal with the flaw.*

Photo Flaw

Undesirable Features of Subject

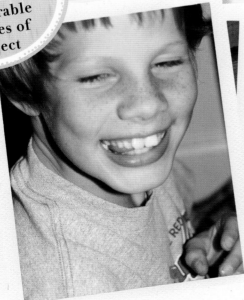

Typically, we want our subjects looking at the camera with pleasant looks on their faces. But more often, photos end up capturing closed eyes and crooked grins. It can be tough to know what to do with a photo that records a memorable event with a less-than-desirable expression.

> ➤ *I have the perfect solution to working with these distractions. Want to know my secret? Turn to page 38.*

Photo Flaw
Poor Framing

Off-center subjects and limbs are common; spontaneous moments don't leave a lot of time to properly frame an image. Often my sour photos are a result of taking photos of my quickly moving kids.

> ► *Sometimes you just have to use what you've got. Find out how on page 18.*

Photo Flaw
Background Distraction

Backgrounds can be full of distractions that often can't be avoided. When we don't have time to clear the background of clutter before we snap a shot, these distractions may take away from the focus of our photo.

> ► *No need to toss those photos! There are several ways to salvage photos with distractions. Check out pages 88-91 to fix your photos digitally.*

Photo Flaw

Poor Lighting

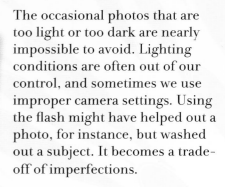

The occasional photos that are too light or too dark are nearly impossible to avoid. Lighting conditions are often out of our control, and sometimes we use improper camera settings. Using the flash might have helped out a photo, for instance, but washed out a subject. It becomes a trade-off of imperfections.

> ▶ *Even if you can't fix the photo, don't give up on using it! Page 60 shows you how to sweeten this sour photo with good design.*

Photo Flaw

Subjects That Are Too Far Away

Like me, you probably have a lot of photos from the days before your zoom lens. Even cameras with a good zoom lens produce photos with subjects that are too far away. Sometimes you forget to use the lens, or you are just too far from the action.

> ▶ *With a little help, you can easily "zoom" in on far-away shots, even after they're captured. Miraculous? Not quite. Turn to page 48 for the trick.*

Photo Flaw
Age

Faded colors, grain and other imperfections from older photos are often due to the lack of quality film and paper available at the time. Imperfections such as scratches and wrinkles can also be problematic with older photos.

▶ *Most of your old photos probably look like this one, right? Don't despair! Turn to page 78 for tips on using aged photos.*

Photo Flaw
Red-Eye

We all have photos with red-eye, that is, photos in which a subject's irises are red instead of black. The red-eye effect is caused by light from a flash traveling through the iris and illuminating the retina at the interior back of the eye and the camera capturing that redness on film. Modern cameras come equipped with a setting that helps prevent the appearance of red-eye within photos, but if this setting is not used, problems arise. Red-eye is a common flaw with older photos taken when this camera setting was not an option.

▶ *It's clear you can't crop out red-eye. But you can clear it up! Learn how to click red-eye away on page 86.*

sweet
(feet)

It doesn't get much sweeter than an adorable
pair of baby feet, especially when they're all
mine! I must have a million photos of your little toes,
but I just can't resist them. Brady · 6/2007

Try Old-Fashioned Recipes

Traditional ways to make flawed photos work

Making lemonade out of those sour photos doesn't have to be fancy or complicated. There's nothing that says new technology is always the best way to sweeten up photos for your layouts. Tapping into traditional methods can go a long way toward solving many of your photo flaws. Some of the solutions are simple ways of fixing up photos— like creative cropping and reducing size—while others are just clever ways of using the photos as is. So no need to pucker up just yet. Let's discuss all the sweet solutions for minimizing, disguising and working with your lemons.

Embrace the Flaws

Look more closely at your "bad" photos. They may turn out to be the perfect ones to use on a page. Through the years I've learned that sometimes photos that don't tell the story I intended actually end up telling a better, more accurate story. A Christmas shot with half-open eyes and crooked smiles, despite cut-off heads, can reveal a lot more than a perfectly posed holiday portrait. So if I come across a photo that at first glance looks like it goes in the "toss" pile, I try to take a second look with a different eye and see how it would work on a page in all its imperfect glory.

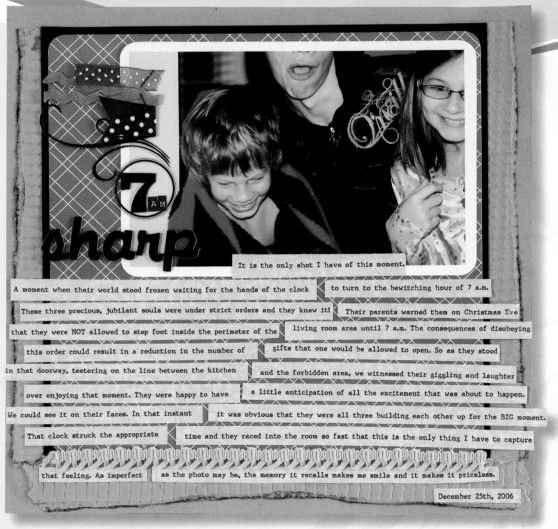

7 AM

sharp

It is the only shot I have of this moment.

A moment when their world stood frozen waiting for the hands of the clock to turn to the bewitching hour of 7 a.m.

These three precious, jubilant souls were under strict orders and they knew it! Their parents warned them on Christmas Eve that they were NOT allowed to step foot inside the perimeter of the living room area until 7 a.m. The consequences of disobeying this order could result in a reduction in the number of gifts that one would be allowed to open. So as they stood in that doorway, teetering on the line between the kitchen and the forbidden area, we witnessed their giggling and laughter over enjoying that moment. They were happy to have a little anticipation of all the excitement that was about to happen. We could see it on their faces. In that instant it was obvious that they were all three building each other up for the BIG moment. That clock struck the appropriate time and they raced into the room so fast that this is the only thing I have to capture that feeling. As imperfect as the photo may be, the memory it recalls makes me smile and it makes it priceless.

December 25th, 2006

The photo on this page clearly cuts a portion of my son's head out of the photo. This spontaneous Christmas morning moment happened so quickly and was over faster than was possible for me to set up the shot correctly. This photo, however, is so priceless that I was compelled to create a layout despite the flaws. I used the photo as is and wrote about the spontaneity in my journaling.

Supplies: Cardstock; patterned paper (Scenic Route); chipboard letters, felt number (American Crafts); letter stickers (Karen Foster); transparency (Hambly); Misc: ribbon

Kelly really knows how to make her photos shine. As you can see, her niece's head is cut off in the photo, but that didn't stop Kelly from creating a fantastic design that captures the exuberance these girls were feeling one afternoon. You can almost hear their giggles as they skip across the yard.

Artwork by *Kelly Noel*

Supplies: Cardstock; patterned paper (Scenic Route); buttons, chipboard letters, ribbon (American Crafts); Misc: Kayleigh font, floss

SpinNiNg
Wheel

when I saw this picture I couldn't help but start to think about how much of your life is like a spinning wheel!...

constantly in motion without a clear begining or end. You have so much going on in your little 10 year old

life that it amazes me how you keep that wheel moving so smoothly. Straight A's at school, Student Council member,

ten hours of dance a week, competitions on the weekends fill up your life. I am so proud of the tremendous

ability that you have to keep all the wheels in your life spinning smoothly...love Mom 2007

My daughter and I have so much fun doing little photo shoots together. Whenever we have a session, I am left with a few outtakes like this one with my daughter's head cut off. Instead of tossing out the photo, I took the opportunity to create a layout focused on the words rather than the photo. Imperfect photos are a great excuse to create layouts expressing sentiment or advice.

Supplies: Cardstock; patterned paper (Fancy Pants); chipboard letters (Heidi Swapp); letter stickers (American Crafts); chipboard accents (Fancy Pants); rhinestones (Martha Stewart); Misc: acrylic paint

What a fun way to incorporate the blurry photos Kimber took of her kids horsing around on a rainy day! When I see the title, I just know these kids were having a great time, and I don't see the blur as an imperfection. If Kimber had looked at these photos and decided they were too blurry for a page, we might have missed this slice of life.

Artwork by *Kimber McGray*

Supplies: Cardstock; patterned paper (Creative Imaginations, Scenic Route); letter stickers (American Crafts); chipboard accents (Fancy Pants); Misc: ink, staples

My son Fletcher made "fingers" out of paper and started making silly gestures. It was a classic Fletcher moment. Even though the photos were blurry, I felt they were a true depiction of this active boy.

Supplies: Digital brushes, patterned paper by Rhonna Farrer (Two Peas in a Bucket)

THIS is what they do.

Ella runs off.
Aaron does his own thing.
Alex is oblivious.
and Abby...
she tries to hold it
all together.
Typical.

Janet used this flawed photo as the perfect opportunity to record the real-life family moment that occurs when trying to capture her four children on film. This "imperfect" photo tells us much more about the family than the perfect portrait Janet was trying to get.

Artwork by *Janet Ohlson*

Supplies: Cardstock; letter stickers, patterned paper (American Crafts); transparency (Hambly)

Hillary normally has the time to set up a shot for great results. When she took these photos, she was in too much of a hurry to capture the important moment to make sure she didn't overexpose her son or keep the distractions out of the foreground. Typically, she would have digitally cropped out and edited the flaws, but she realized while making this page that the imperfections added to the charm and context of the moment.

Artwork by *Hillary Heidelberg*

Supplies: Cardstock; letter stickers (Doodlebug); chipboard tile (Die Cuts with a View); brads (Bazzill); Misc: Rockwell font

ReAD

So we'd been 'practicing' reading for a while, learning letters, sounding out words, and reading to you a lot. But whenever I suggested you read a book by yourself, you would balk. "But Mo-ooom, why can't *you* just read meeee the book???"you'd moan. So anyway, one morning I am making breakfast for you boys and some Bob books are on the dining room table. You're absent-mindedly shuffling through them, and you say to me "Is this about a lion?" "Looks like it. Why don't you read it?" I respond, fully expecting you to ignore me. But guess what? You read it. The whole thing, all about the lion and the vet who fixes his bad leg. I just stayed in the kitchen the whole time as you read out loud, not wanting you to see how excited I was. And I was very, very excited....GOOD JOB, LUCA!!

(09.18.07)

I ♥ U

Didn't
SEE
that
Coming...

ABBY CATCHES JACOB OFF GUARD IN A COMPLETELY NON POSED AND UNPLANNED MOMENT.

I WAS PLAYING WITH THE SETTINGS WITH MY CAMERA WHEN I CAUGHT THIS SHOT.

ABBY IS STILL WATCHING TV AS SHE TAKES A SWIPE AT HER BROTHER. CHARMING.

MAY 2007.

Artwork by *Nic Howard*

Nic captured the spirit of her kids' interaction so wonderfully on this page. Her clever journaling allows the reader to take a peek at a "real" moment in their life. How many times have we snapped a photo like this with lots of blur and just deleted it off our camera because it was clearly flawed? This layout shows us how beautifully we can display a "flawed" memory.

Supplies: Cardstock; patterned paper (My Mind's Eye, Rouge de Garance, Scenic Route); letters (American Crafts, Scenic Route); chipboard accent (Deluxe Designs); Misc: Tasklist font

Focus on the Story

We wouldn't scrapbook if we didn't have stories to tell. So why not take advantage of them? Whether you take the focus off imperfections by putting your journaling in the spotlight or even explaining the photo's flaws on the page, focusing on the story is a simple way to accept and use a photo as it is.

My kids and I spent a wonderful week with my mom and dad in the summer of 2007, but I don't have any photos to show for it. The one photo that my mom took was on her camera phone at the baseball game she went to with my children. As you can see, the kids are far away in the photo, and it's really pixilated. Still, I felt compelled to take this photo and create a page all about the journaling to share my mom's thoughts about that week we enjoyed together. The title really says it all!

Supplies: Cardstock; letters (Everlasting Keepsakes, Heidi Swapp); Misc: Arial font, glitter

I look at this portrait and see myself sitting there trying to suck in my stomach. I also see my son torturing his brother. This photo isn't imperfect because of camera flaws, but it still has flaws. So I used words to call attention to a family moment that was blissfully typical. The fonts give the words a punch that makes the story the focus.

Supplies: Cardstock; die-cut strips, patterned paper (My Mind's Eye); letter stickers (American Crafts); Misc: 2Peas Sidewalk, Blazing and Typedenski fonts

Even when your photo isn't so bad, you can use a story to enhance it. When I read Janet's journaling, I realized there was more than meets the eye in the photo. Her words bring the photo to life. Without them, I wouldn't have known about all the behind-the-scenes activity, nor would I have realized Janet's feelings. I'm glad she took the time to enhance a basic photo with meaningful words.

Artwork by *Janet Ohlson*

Supplies: Digital paper by Dana Zarling (Designer Digitals); brush by Jesse Edwards (Designer Digitals); Misc: Avant Garde font

Explore *Family* Dream Create Love

The Story

Every year Uncle Jack throws a hum-dinger of
a Pig Roast. The event is officially in
honor of Jack's birthday, his 60th this year,
but it's really just a great excuse to gather
family and friends at the lake in Antioch.
We have always enjoyed nice weather,
that is ... until this year. It was dark and
wet. It literally rained all day long.
But everyone did their best to ignore the
unusually damp weather and just enjoy
the picnic. After a full day of playing
in the rain,you would have thought
everyone would be heading home early.
Nope. when the night took over, Aunt Karen
brought out boxes and boxes of giant
sparklers. Grandma Carol and
Great Grandpa Jack stood for a good hour
lighting all the sparklers for the kids.
Since this was the first family gathering
following Great Grandma's death, we just
weren't sure if Great Grandpa would be up
for celebrating. It is true he experienced
tearful moments throughout the day, but this
picture (while not the greatest of quality and
clarity) speaks volumes.
Great Grandpa just keeps on ...
even when it is hard.

My friend Connie had such an incredibly
moving story to accompany this photo, I
felt compelled to place the emphasis on
the journaling when I created the page. It
tells the story of family members getting
together and enjoying one another, in
spite of bad weather and personal loss.
The words help the strength of the
subjects come through loud and clear in
the photo, even though their faces glow
with redness. This design allows the
page to clearly explain what family bonds
mean to Connie.

Supplies: Cardstock; patterned paper, sticker accents (Rusty Pickle); brads (Fiskars); Misc: Old Typewriter font

Nic shared the story behind this
layout, and it made my heart melt.
While she was trying to set up a
home photo studio, her daughter
picked up her camera and began
snapping away. Nic took this photo as
an opportunity to journal about her
relationship with her middle child.
The spontaneous photo taken by her
three-year-old wasn't exactly picture
perfect, but the journaling helped
create a perfectly heartwarming page.

Artwork by *Nic Howard*

calm
in the
day

Supplies: Die-cut labels, patterned paper (Scenic Route); chipboard letters (CherryArte); rub-ons (Adornit, BasicGrey); chipboard accents (Jenni Bowlin, Scenic Route); transparency (Hambly); Misc: Pea Shirley font, ink, ribbon

3 TIMES a CHARM

Jacob & Fletcher
1st Carolina Hurricanes game
Winter 2005

My boys went to their first Major league hockey game with strict instructions to take lots of photos. When they returned, I found these two photos on the memory card. THAT'S IT? It took 3 games later before I got decent shots of them at the game

What you don't see in these photos is what my boys experienced at their first pro hockey game—that's the flaw. I was disappointed with the photos (or lack thereof) when they returned home, and I let these lone images sit in a drawer. But after some time had passed, I realized that the story was actually quite humorous, and so it became the starting point for my layout.

Supplies: Cardstock; patterned paper (CherryArte, Junkitz); chipboard letters (Heidi Swapp); chipboard accent (Li'l Davis); conchos (Making Memories); journaling card (Luxe); Misc: glitter, paint

Highlight the Positive

Often, the majority of a photo is perfectly sweet with just one or two flaws turning it into a lemon. With photos like these— which usually have a few background distractions or lots of open space around a subject—you can highlight the best part of a photo by using creative framing.

COUSIN

CONNECTION

Fletcher & Michael

They are only 6months apart in age and love to do regular boy things together. We don't get to spend time together very often but when we do, they don't miss a beat.

family

Memories

Supplies: Cardstock; patterned paper (Fontwerks, Scenic Route); chipboard letters (Scenic Route); sticker accents (7gypsies, Creative Imaginations); transparency (Hambly); brads (Bazzill); Misc: ribbon

When I first looked at this photo of my nephew and my son, my eye kept getting pulled to the clutter behind them. While I wanted to focus on the boys, I felt the signs of boyhood in the background were an important part of the story. So, to minimize the background but allow it to remain visible, I layered the photo with a printed transparency. You can still see the evidence that these two were having fun, but your focus is on the relationship between them.

gReen
THUMB

This photo was taken in the early 90's at the start of Jason's landscape career. It amazes me to see how far he... has come

My husband, Jason, is a horticulturist and landscape architect, and it is a big part of who he is as a person. I found this older photo of him from when he first began working in the industry, and I felt the background was an important context. So, instead of enlarging the photo so Jason would be closer, I left the background visible and used a small metal frame to draw attention directly to the subject.

*Supplies: Cardstock; patterned paper (KI Memories);
letter stickers (American Crafts, Mustard Moon);
metal accent (Making Memories); journaling card
(Fontwerks); Misc: ribbon*

A Starry Night

6-07

The tradition continues! Bill has always been into the outdoors and I grew up camping as our family vacations. Andrew and Bill had their 1st camping experience. Bill dug out his old tent and pitched it in the back yard. Out came the sleeping bags and pillows. We grabbed the flashlights and some books. Andrew was ready to go in his Buzz Lightyear jammies. One last thing to grab. A kiss and a hug from me and "Bun-bun" to cuddle up with in the tent. After a few questions he was out like a light.

Artwork by *Kimber McGray*

Kimber's son had his first campout in a tent in their backyard. Look how precious he looks in that tent with the glow of the light on him! It's a perfect memory that photo flaws—like blurriness and bad lighting—can't take away. Kimber used a simple frame to both outline the center of her design and hide a portion of the photo. The creative framing highlights the special moment, and downplays the distractions.

Supplies: Cardstock; patterned paper (American Crafts); letter stickers (Making Memories); chipboard accents (Fancy Pants)

This is one of my all-time-favorite photos of Fletcher because it perfectly captures a slice of his personality. He was into skating and hockey at an early age. To bring the focus to the star of the photo, I fit journaling over the empty space beside Fletcher, highlighting him in the way the words fit around his body. I also used digital brushes and embellishments to disguise the blank wall on the other side and complete the frame around my son.

Supplies: Digital star brushes, page kit by Rhonna Farrer (Two Peas in a Bucket); circle brushes by Sande Krieger (Two Peas in a Bucket)

Mask Imperfections

Embellishments are like the jewelry of a scrapbook page. They dress it up—and they can also work wonders for sprucing up flawed photos. A well-placed embellishment, combined with good design, can enhance a layout and make an otherwise imperfect photo look fabulous.

I'm always so proud of my daughter's accomplishments at school. When I took this photo, I wanted Madison to be the focus in the photo despite her being in a group. To achieve this, I placed an embellishment cluster over the section of the photo that would detract from my daughter. The result is a layout that brings your eye right to Madison.

Supplies: Cardstock; patterned paper (KI Memories, Scenic Route); letter stickers (American Crafts); chipboard letters (Scenic Route); chipboard shapes (Everlasting Keepsakes); decorative tape, transparency (Hambly); Misc: mesh

Linda took this photo of her son to capture the expression on his face, but the light above his head was distracting. Linda used the conversation bubble as a unique way to both include her journaling and cover up the light.

Artwork by *Linda Harrison*

Supplies: Cardstock; letter stickers (Adornit); plastic letters (Heidi Swapp); brads (Making Memories); sticker accents (Me & My Big Ideas); chipboard accent (One Heart One Mind); rub-ons (K&Co.); text bubble by Pattie Knox (Designer Digitals); Misc: Times New Roman font, paint

It's clear in the original photo that my friend's two sons were having a blast in the snow. But, perhaps it's not as clear as she would have liked considering the huge falling snowflakes. To bring the focus back on the boys, I simply added a snowflake embellishment over the snowy blobs.

Supplies: Cardstock; die-cut title, patterned paper (My Mind's Eye); rub-ons (7gypsies); acrylic snowflakes (Making Memories); Misc: conchos, spray paint

If you saw this layout in a magazine or even in real life, chances are you would never have guessed that Kelly considered this photo imperfect. I honestly couldn't believe what a terrific job she did concealing the distraction. Her title treatment works perfectly to create a layout design that focuses directly on those "sweet feet."

Artwork by *Kelly Noel*

Supplies: Cardstock; patterned paper (KI Memories); heart accent, letters, ribbon (American Crafts); buttons (Autumn Leaves); Misc: SP Wonderful Wendy font

This photo is a classic example of a distraction in the background. The house and the car were not so pretty, and I needed a way to bring the focus to this gorgeous shot of my daughter. So, I easily disguised the distraction using ribbon and patterned paper that draw the eye right to Madison's face.

Supplies: Cardstock; patterned paper (American Crafts, Creative Imaginations, KI Memories); rub-on letters and accents (Scenic Route, Urban Lily); word sticker (Heidi Swapp); ribbon (Sweetwater)

Suzy's style always has a burst of the unexpected. She continues to amaze me with her design skills with this clever embellishment cover-up. The result is a fun, funky layout that puts the focus on her daughter rather than on the background. It's a lesson that we should consider all sorts of possibilities when we are disguising distractions.

Supplies: Cardstock; chipboard buttons, letter stickers, patterned paper, ribbon, sticker accents (KI Memories); Misc: ink

Artwork by *Suzy Plantamura*

I was not yet alive when John F. Kennedy was assassinated. I grew up knowing that it was in Dallas, but even though I lived 30 miles away, never had any curiosity about seeing the place where it happened. Last month, on our vacation home, I finally walked around the "grassy knoll" and saw the Schoolbook Depository building and all the memorials in downtown Dallas. It was more moving than I had thought it would be...it was history come to life, and I'm glad I took the time to walk around, to remember the old news stories...to pay my respects. History is history, whether I was alive for it or not.

August 2007

history.

Janet's page perfectly illustrates how masking can hide distraction as well as pull the journaling into the design of the page. Instead of cropping out the people in the photo, Janet typed her journaling in a semi-transparent box placed over that part of the image. Janet added a digital journaling block, but you can achieve the same effect with handwriting on vellum. I like how she didn't have to crop out a portion of the building that has special meaning to her.

Artwork by *Janet Ohlson*

Supplies: Digital brushes and paper by Anna Aspnes (Designer Digitals); graphic edge brush by Katie Pertiet (Designer Digitals); Misc: Suede and Times New Roman fonts

Fletcher, of course! After all, it is at his house but he is good about sharing with other people like our neighbor Marcus. Their favorite things to do include... Dunking, racing, backflips and general horseplay. Who really rules the pool is the Fun! Fletcher and Marcus horsing around Aug. 07

Who RULES THE POOL

One of a photographer's worst nightmares is a distracting background that can't just be moved. Here, overlapping the various photos easily concealed most of the unattractive backyard mess behind the subjects. The journaling strips hid the rest.

Supplies: Cardstock; patterned paper (CherryArte); letters (Doodlebug, Heidi Swapp); chipboard shapes (Everlasting Keepsakes); sticker accents (Creative Imaginations)

Unfortunately, many of my grandmother's photos were lost so the few I have are very precious to me. These photos were taken when my mom was pregnant with me, so despite the damage they've incurred, they compelled me to use them on a layout. I didn't want to crop out any portions of the photos that gave a little peek into Mom's life back then, so I camouflaged the imperfections and background distractions using transparencies.

Supplies: Cardstock; patterned paper, sticker accents (7gypsies); transparency (My Mind's Eye); pin (Making Memories)

Crop Out Flaws

I can't begin to tell you how many shots I've taken where one person had his or her head turned, while other individuals in the photo were picture perfect. What is clearly a flawed photo can actually be salvaged using a few simple tricks. Cropping is a great option for saving these types of photos, eliminating bad parts altogether and refocusing the attention.

Here, you can see that my son's eyes are closed, but that devilish grin is unmistakably perfect for telling the story. Cropping out the photo imperfection—closed eyes—allows the message to come through loud and clear. In the design, I highlighted the disappearing ink with a circle, and the journaling ties it all together.

Supplies: Cardstock; patterned paper (Crate Paper, Making Memories); rub-on letters (Daisy D's, Fontwerks); transparency (Hambly); Misc: Bradley Hand font

be her guiding LIGHT

In this photo, I intended to capture the perfect family portrait. Obviously, I failed to achieve that. But the portion of the photo with my daughter and son was perfect for a page about their relationship, one I probably wouldn't have thought to create otherwise. When looking at a lemon photo, don't just look at the picture as a whole. Take it in parts, looking for salvageable sections.

Supplies: Die-cut shapes, patterned paper (Crate Paper); chipboard letters (American Crafts, Pressed Petals); rub-on letters (Li'l Davis); chipboard accent (Everlasting Keepsakes); Misc: Times New Roman font

Every year you get this look on your face that signals

Fletcher
DATE Sept '06

The hours spent in the sun are spellbinding

I look forward to this look

magic of SHINE

This photo of my son's face taken on the deck of a beach house captured the essence of our summer. However, his arm reaching up in a distracting way took away from the overall mood, so I simply cropped the picture close on my son's head.

Supplies: Digital patterned paper (Designer Digitals); graph brush, stamped accents, sun prints by Katie Pertiet (Designer Digitals); date stamp, epoxy accent, oval tag, swirls by Rhonna Farrer (Two Peas in a Bucket)

Lucie with Grandma Jo-Ann
We loved watching little Lucie's reaction to the bubbles her Daddy was blowing.
Summer 2007

pretty princess

When my friend Robin shared these photos of her niece, she knew there was a really sweet photo behind the background distractions. A little cropping and layering brought the focus directly on that sweet little girl. I chose a pink and light turquoise blue color combination to lend the page softness and innocence. And since the colors were pulled from the photo, the pictures really pop.

Supplies: Cardstock; patterned paper (Dream Street); die-cut title, transparency (My Mind's Eye); chipboard accent (Everlasting Keepsakes); Misc: glitter, paint

buddies

BRYCE

AIDAN

CONNOR

Cousins just hanging out, having fun together at the family Wedding/Summer 2007

This layout shows just how much a super-simple fix can change the look of a photo. My friend Robin showed me this photo of her son and her nephews, and she asked if there was anything I could do to fix the problem—the half of someone else in the photo was too distracting. I simply cropped around the center of the photo where my subjects are, allowing their relationship to shine on the layout.

Supplies: Cardstock; patterned paper (Daisy D's, Dude Designs, Luxe); acrylic letters (Junkitz); transparency (My Mind's Eye); Misc: Bookman Old Style font

Use Open Space

In the past, I would look at a photo with an expanse of background around my subject and immediately have the urge to crop it. All that would be left was a sliver of a photo and the remnants of where the picture took place. As time went on, I realized I should have kept the full-size versions of many photos with their backgrounds intact. Even if the subject is off center or a background is a prominent feature of the photo, I've learned to work with the photo flaw by taking advantage of the open space.

As my son was playing his soccer game, he moved toward me faster than I was prepared for, and I didn't have time to center him in the lens. This is the shot I got. I really loved the intensity of how my son looked in this photo, and I figured the open space provided a great place to rest my journaling. By fighting the urge to crop the photo, I added visual interest and meaning to my layout and used a great image that might have otherwise been considered unworthy.

Supplies: Cardstock; patterned paper (CherryArte); letter stickers (American Crafts); chipboard letters (Imagination Project)

go go go

it's a big, big world, and you're a little girl... yet I have no doubt that you will have no difficulty meeting this world head-on.

love, mommy

Artwork by *Janet Ohlson*

Janet's layout shows how you can not only embrace open space but make it the focus of a layout. I was touched by the journaling and how it related to the vast amount of space around Janet's little girl. Janet also cleverly used the steps in the park to provide a guide for her writing. This helped incorporate elements from the open space into the page design to add visual interest.

Supplies: Cardstock; chipboard letters, patterned paper (American Crafts); chipboard accents (Maya Road); transparency (Hambly); Misc: acrylic paint

it was on this island that we made our
TURNING POINT

we came to north carolina to determine if we should move our family here and were unable to make a decision up to this point in our trip.

we came here and it all became clear...this is where we were meant to be there was something magical about being on this island that gave us the clarity to move the thousand miles from illinois. a pivotal moment in our life took place here and i will never forget how important this trip became to us

jason & sherry

Aug 2001

This layout is a great example of the impact that incorporating open space can have. The peace and solitude of this island helped my husband and I arrive at our decision to move a thousand miles from our family and friends. These photos, with all their open space, help tell that story and convey the impact this trip had on us. The photos' similar backgrounds also contribute to the sense that there is just one photo in the layout, which is something I wanted to achieve when I created this page.

Supplies: Digital overlay (Two Peas in a Bucket); stamp brushes by Rhonna Farrer (Two Peas in a Bucket); Misc: Think Small font

This photo is such a perfect metaphor for my relationship with my daughter. She's constantly running away while I try to call her back. And it's a big, scary world that she's running away to, and I'm afraid she'll get in over her head. As on the day I took this photo, I can only hope and pray that she stays safe in that big world.

runaway

photo october 2005
journaling june 2007

I love how Janet took this photo with all its vast amount of open space to create a layout that sends a message to her daughter. The open space is incorporated into the design and helps bring home the message of her daughter running away, literally and figuratively. She emphasizes her daughter's image with the square but still leaves the visual of openness around her.

Artwork by *Janet Ohlson*

Supplies: Digital brush frame, paper by Katie Pertiet (Designer Digitals); Misc: Geo Sans Light and Impact fonts

solo swim

and then one day.... it happened. You decided you would try to swim without your floatie. But part of you didn't really want to, and I didn't want to push. So I said, why not just swim over to me? I am only a bit away. And you said okay. And you did it. You swam. And then, you swam some more. And then you jumped off the side of the pool and swam to me, and I was halfway across the pool And you were so amazingly proud of yourself. Five years old. Swimming solo. I am so proud of you for overcoming your fears. Luca (08.07)

Just prior to this shot, Hillary's son was holding onto the side of the pool, and she jumped out to grab her camera. Moments later, she turned around and snapped this photo without having time to compose a great shot. Of course she still wanted to scrapbook this less-than-perfect photo, so, she incorporated the background into the page design by simply adding a decorative rub-on. It's stories like these—with great memories and not-so-great photos—that inspired me to write this book!

Supplies: Cardstock; brads, patterned paper, rub-on swirls (We R Memory Keepers); chipboard letters (American Crafts); Misc: Tully font

Artwork by *Hillary Heidelberg*

THE

bored

board

My little man having a moment.
With his surfboard...

The waves were just a bit too rough that day,
and you were finding it tough to surf. I caught
you at this moment having some alone time.

A single solitary moment of boredom.
Lucky for us all, it was brief and you were back
on your board doing what you do best...

Fletcher 2006

Fletcher looked less than thrilled at this moment, and I remember thinking as I took that photo what a rare sight it was to see Fletcher looking this way. I knew I needed to scrapbook what many wouldn't know just by looking at this photo by itself. In the before photo, you can see the space to the left of Fletcher. Using that space to incorporate the journaling and embellishing was the perfect solution to both keeping and filling the space.

Supplies: Cardstock; patterned paper (Dream Street, KI Memories, Scenic Route, SEI); chipboard letters (Heidi Swapp, Scenic Route); letter stickers (Doodlebug); chipboard accents (Everlasting Keepsakes, Heidi Swapp); transparency (Hambly); Misc: acrylic paint

Enlarge Photos with Faraway Subjects

Back in the days of my old film camera, I had to take photos without the aid of a zoom lens. As you can imagine, I took many photos where my children were swallowed up by their surroundings. I discovered a trick for creating zoom after a photo has already been captured. It is most effective when you can crop out the background around the subject. If you enlarge a photo to 8" × 10" (20cm × 25cm) or larger and then crop that photo to a smaller size, your subject instantly becomes larger—and perfect for a page.

FINDING

BURIED treasure

You never know what you will find while digging in the sand. On this particular day at the beach, Fletcher and his friend Austin Brooks started searching in the sand for hermit crabs. Curiosity made Madison join them. This led to a seashell hunt and a sand castle build. Good things happen when you dig.

2007

Even though I own a pretty nice zoom lens, it's only capable of zooming in so far. On this particular day at the beach, I happened to take a little stroll and spotted the kids intently digging in the sand. I was fascinated and wanted to capture them, but as you can see in the before photo, I didn't get close enough. I used my trick of enlarging the photo and cropping out the background, and I'm pleased with the result.

Supplies: Cardstock; patterned paper (7gypsies, Daisy D's, Sassafras Lass); letter stickers (Making Memories); chipboard letters (Heidi Swapp, Li'l Davis); chipboard accent (Everlasting Keepsakes); brads (Making Memories); die-cut tag (Sassafras Lass); Misc: mesh, twine

what

a

disappointment

to

grab

a

wave

only

to

have

it

fizzle

out

catchin a wave

HUH?

IS THAT IT?

there's always the next one, buddy!

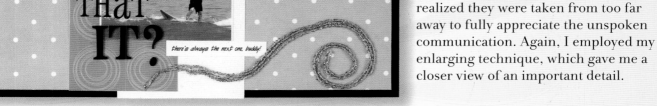

I had no idea when I was shooting my son on his surfboard that this hilarious scene was about to take place. The arm gestures just seemed to say it all. I couldn't wait to scrapbook these photos, but when I loaded them, I realized they were taken from too far away to fully appreciate the unspoken communication. Again, I employed my enlarging technique, which gave me a closer view of an important detail.

Supplies: Cardstock; patterned paper (Dream Street, Dude Designs); letter stickers (Mustard Moon); chipboard letters (Heidi Swapp); Misc: glitter fibers

This particular day was such an important one for my husband and his family. At the time, we didn't own a nice camera with a quality zoom lens, and the result was low-quality photos. We were seated really far from the stage, making it nearly impossible to get a good shot. Since these are the only photos of that day, I cherish them despite their flaws. I worked around the lack of zoom by enlarging the photo and cropping it to focus on the graduates.

Supplies: Cardstock; letter stickers, patterned paper (BasicGrey); chipboard accents (Everlasting Keepsakes, Imagination Project); Misc: corkboard, ink

GRADUATION

from

Illinois Central College

What an incredible day it was to watch Jason graduate from college in 1995. This accomplishment was one that had never occurred in his family by any anyone else.

Getting a degree in Horticulture gave him the basis for the career that he has worked in for the past 15 years.

He went on to begin his own business in 2005 and continues to run his business today.

Remember Today

Reduce the Size

We often hear that bigger is better. This is not necessarily the case when it comes to imperfect photos. Enlarging a photo can make photo "noise"—like distortion, blurring and pixilation—appear more prominent. Reducing the size of a photograph hides the noise and allows a bad photo to work on a page. The smaller the photo, the closer together the pixels are, and the clearer the photo will appear. Try using photos smaller than 4" × 6" (10cm × 15cm) to achieve the best results.

Mark and
Yvonne Schwartz

Renew their
vows at
Blessed Sacrament
church in 1980

My parents renewed their vows when I was too small to remember. Even though this photo is grainy, I still love how it captures their renewed commitment. Reducing this photo to 3" × 5" (8cm × 13cm) makes the photo look less grainy. This increased quality breathes new life into the photo and allows the viewer to appreciate the moment without distraction.

Supplies: Cardstock; patterned paper (A2Z, Chatterbox, Doodlebug, Hambly); rub-on letters (7gypsies); metal word (Making Memories); chipboard ampersand (American Crafts); chipboard circles (Everlasting Keepsakes); Misc: Times New Roman font, ink

Kelly did a fabulous job of disguising the blurriness in these adorable photos of her son by reducing their size to less than 3" (8cm) high. The result is a fabulous layout that shows off the bubble action without the distraction.

Artwork by *Kelly Noel*

Supplies: Cardstock; brads, patterned paper (American Crafts); chipboard letters (Heidi Swapp); Misc: AL Serenade font

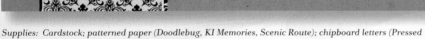

My grandparents lived in Florida nearly my whole life. I didn't get the opportunity to see them very often, but when we did, a trip to Disney was on the agenda. This amusement park holds many memories of family time and happiness. I

rarely think of one without the other. Even though it has been over 20 years since I visited Disney with my grandparents, I still can almost hear the laughter and joy when I look at this photo. *Photo taken in the early '70s*

MY grandparents

This photo brings back memories of my youth with my grandparents. The colors in the photo are starting to fade, but the expressions remain priceless. Rather than filling this layout with an enlarged photo, which would have blown up the photo's imperfections, I simply used a 3.5" × 5" (9cm × 13cm) version and completed the page with large title letters and lots of journaling.

Supplies: Cardstock; patterned paper (Doodlebug, KI Memories, Scenic Route); chipboard letters (Pressed Petals); letter stickers (American Crafts); transparency (Hambly)

When I took these photos, it was almost sunset. It is the perfect time for skateboarding, but not for photographing a skateboarder. Of course, despite the flaws, I still wanted to capture the action on a scrapbook page. I let the sweetest photo take center stage and reduced the size of the other photos to minimize the blur.

Supplies: Cardstock; patterned paper (BasicGrey); rub-ons (Fontwerks); brads (Making Memories); Misc: Trashco font, acrylic paint, mesh

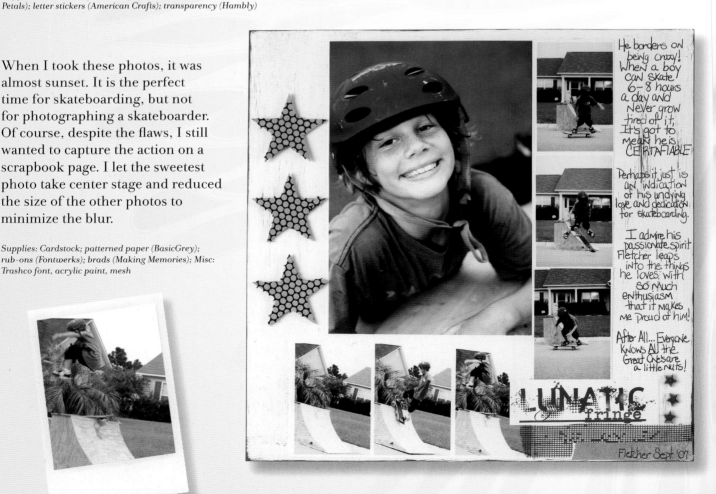

He borders on being crazy! When a boy can skate 6-8 hours a day and never grow tired of it, it's got to mean he is CERTIFIABLE.

Perhaps it just is an indication of his undying love and dedication for skateboarding.

I admire his passionate spirit. Fletcher leaps into the things he loves with so much enthusiasm that it makes me proud of him!

After all... Everyone knows all the Great Ones are a little nuts!

LUNATIC fringe

Fletcher Sept '07

This layout is a classic example of trying to capture my active son. In the main photo (featuring that sneaky smile!) everything but his face is blurred, so I used that one to star on the layout. Then I reduced the size of the other blurry photos to both direct focus on the good photo and minimize the blur.

Supplies: Cardstock; patterned paper (BasicGrey, Scenic Route); letters (American Crafts, Doodlebug); brads (Bazzill)

2

Not once, not twice but, every time Laura was asked what she wanted to ride at the fair. "The horses" is what she requested. We took turns riding with her and if left to her, we would still be riding them. This choice of rides was at the top of the list at Kings Island, too.

Indiana state fair

Round & Round!

August 2007

The girl likes her horses!

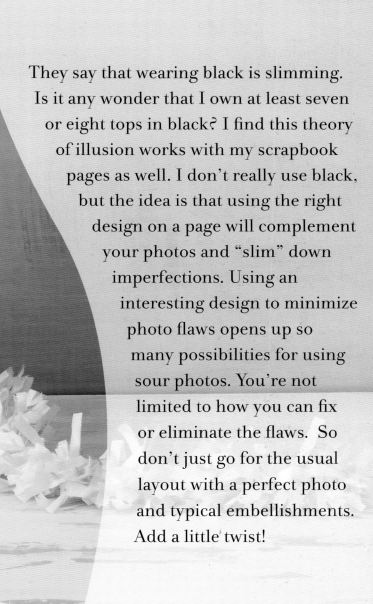

Design with a Twist
Design techniques to sweeten photos

They say that wearing black is slimming. Is it any wonder that I own at least seven or eight tops in black? I find this theory of illusion works with my scrapbook pages as well. I don't really use black, but the idea is that using the right design on a page will complement your photos and "slim" down imperfections. Using an interesting design to minimize photo flaws opens up so many possibilities for using sour photos. You're not limited to how you can fix or eliminate the flaws. So don't just go for the usual layout with a perfect photo and typical embellishments. Add a little twist!

Design with Color

You can use color on a layout in a variety of ways to enhance a photo or disguise its flaws. Use color to brighten dark and dreary photos. Use color to draw attention away from flaws. Or use color when photos clash.

I bet everyone has birthday photos like these in their stash. The perfect way to capture my son blowing out his candles was to turn out the lights. Taking photos in the dark is never a great idea, but in this case it was required. Try to use lighter backgrounds and brighter colors to balance out darker photos. It was easy to do with this fun, boyish birthday page.

Supplies: Cardstock; patterned paper (Scenic Route); rub-on letters and accents (7gypsies); brads (Bazzill); chipboard stars (Everlasting Keepsakes); buttons (Doodlebug); ribbon (American Crafts); Misc: Angelia font, paint

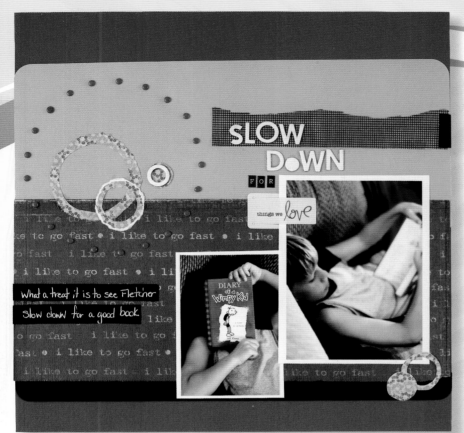

When I caught Fletcher reading this book, I wanted to document a rare moment of my son taking it slow. I did edit the photos to brighten them up, but what really makes the layout work are the blocks of bright colors that enliven the page. The red background and brads both bring out the vivid color of the book in the photo.

Supplies: Cardstock; patterned paper (Crate Paper); chipboard letters (Doodlebug); letter stickers (Making Memories); plastic tag (Heidi Swapp); brads (Bazzill)

Red, pink, purple and . . . camouflage? Suzy puzzled over what colors to work with on this layout, and who can blame her? But Suzy's such a pro that she pulled off a stellar layout by simply focusing on two of the complementary colors: pink and red. The result is a fabulous combination that pulls out color from the photos. Her trick works so well I hardly even notice the camouflage.

Artwork by *Suzy Plantamura*

Supplies: Cardstock; letter stickers, patterned paper, ribbon, rub-ons, sticker accents (KI Memories)

Create Energy and Movement

Elements that create energy and movement redirect a viewer's eye. Energy—formed by interesting designs, bright colors, swirls and similar design elements—grabs a viewer's attention and helps draw focus to the design. Movement, whether in the way the photos are arranged or in how design elements are placed, guides viewers to move quickly from one photo or area to the next, keeping eyes from zeroing in on every flaw.

I threw an impromptu birthday party for Jason to celebrate his 37th. I called friends on Monday to come over on Saturday. I was not prepared to have nearly 35 people tell me that they were available to attend. Isn't it funny what happens when you least expect it?

the SMOKE alarm Test

We went shopping for the food and I had to find a birthday cake. The only thing I could find that would serve the number of guests was a cake with bright pink flowers on it. Lucky for me, cake and icing all tastes the same to Jason no matter what color it is. 4/07

I threw my husband a last-minute birthday party, and he was shy about the attention. Since he really didn't want me to take his picture while he was blowing out the candles on his cake, I had to do it quickly. This didn't give me much time to get the settings on my camera right. As a result, I had pretty dark photos. I chose to line them up to create movement across the page. And the background paper—with its spiraling squares—also creates energy, perfect for a birthday page.

Supplies: Cardstock; embellishments, patterned paper (Tinkering Ink); letter stickers (American Crafts); Misc: transparency

Not once, not twice but, every time Laura was asked what she wanted to ride at the fair- "The Horses!" is what she requested. We took turns riding with her and if left to her, we would still be riding them. This choice of rides was at the top of the list at Kings Island, too.
Indiana State Fair
The girl likes her Horses!
Round & Round!
August 2007

When designing this layout, Kimber had to work with busy and blurry photos that were too dark. So she decided to put together a lively design to minimize the photos' flaws. The visual triangle of cheery circles easily moves the eye around the page; the curved lines complement the circles and also create a sense of movement. Kimber infused energy into the design with glittery title letters and a bold green background.

Supplies: Cardstock; patterned paper (American Crafts, Heidi Grace); letter stickers (Making Memories)

Artwork by *Kimber McGray*

Kimber shows us how a smartly designed layout can make her busy little guy's dancing photos shine. Adding the spiral circles infuses the page with energy. And placing the photos on a angle and in a line conveys a series of action, helping us focus on the dancing and not the blur.

Artwork by *Kimber McGray*

Supplies: Cardstock; die-cut letters, felt accents, patterned paper (Tinkering Ink); transparency (Hambly)

I couldn't help but find these flawed photos charming, accurately portraying what happens when your friends sing happy birthday a little off-key. On this layout, vertical strips of paper in vivid colors and interesting patterns bring attention to the design and lead the eye down the page. I matched that look with the placement of my photos, ensuring that any one photo doesn't attract all the attention.

Supplies: Cardstock; patterned paper (Autumn Leaves); letter stickers (American Crafts, EK Success, Making Memories); chipboard ruler (Scenic Route); sticker accents (KI Memories); ribbon (Junkitz); brads (Making Memories)

As I watch the neighborhood girls hang out

with Madison, I can see the

understood language that comes from knowing

each other for a long time

They have been friends since early elementary school

and as they enter middle school, they have

⋄ Samantha James ⋄ Kennedy Pierce ⋄ Madison Steveson ⋄ 'the girlfriends'

remained friends They may have their moments

where they arent as close but that never stops

them from coming back together to hang out

I hope they remain friends for life! Sept 2007

When I saw my daughter's friends standing near her in our doorway, I grabbed my camera. It's those spontaneous moments that are the hardest to set up properly. It's difficult to edit a photo that is both too light and too dark like this one. So I went with a design that provides loads of fun and energy, making the design, and not the poor quality of the photos, the star. Vivid colors, patterns and waves across the spread bring movement and visual interest.

Supplies: Cardstock; die-cut title, patterned paper (My Mind's Eye); Misc: Old Typewriter font

Embrace the Age

Preserving photos to be able to relive the memories is, of course, an important part of why we scrapbook. Unfortunately, you probably find in your own stash vintage photos that have lost a considerable amount of their original color and many that have begun to yellow as a result of too much exposure to light. Guess what? It's okay to leave the photos as they are. Embrace the age! Use the photos on a layout with a design that mimics the look of the photos, ugly colors and all.

This photo of me with my parents became the starting point for a layout about memories of my life in a military family. Using the old photo despite its color flaws, I made an eye-catching layout that highlights memories of my childhood. The colors in this photo screamed vintage, so I played up the look. Now, no one will question my decision to use this yellowed photo—it's the perfect fit for a '70s-inspired design!

Supplies: Cardstock; patterned paper (7gypsies, Chatterbox); chipboard letters (Everlasting Keepsakes); letter stickers (Making Memories); bookplate (7gypsies); Misc: acrylic paint

'70s KID

Nothing was cooler than the '70s!?!
Digging through pictures to see some of my 'style' growing up and the rockin' mushroom shirt ; groovy skates are somethin' to remember!
- Christmas Skate Party 1976 -

Kimber loves looking back at the styles of the '70s in the photos of her youth. This layout is a tribute to that time, and Kimber used a similar design concept to embrace the age in her photo. She used a white background to balance and brighten the dark image, and chose cheery designs with kid-friendly shapes to enhance the theme.

Artwork by *Kimber McGray*

Supplies: Cardstock; patterned paper (Imaginisce, Making Memories); rub-ons (Hambly); paper punch (Stampin' Up); Misc: ink

When Hillary saw this photo of her mother, her first thought was that it illustrated her mom's independence and was a symbol of the adventures she took by herself. Hillary embraced the age of the photo and designed the page, with the photo in the center, to enhance the idea of her mother being the center of attention. She also used soft, worn-looking papers to play up the vintage theme.

Supplies: Digital patterned paper (Holly McCaig, Sugar Giggles); brushes by Katie Pertiet (Designer Digitals) and Rhonna Farrer (Two Peas in a Bucket); title letter by Katie Pertiet (Designer Digitals); Misc: Kunstler Script and Uncle Charles fonts

my mom

Looking so very fashionable while travelling in Hong Kong. Always up for an adventure. 1973

Artwork by *Hillary Heidelberg*

Design around the Flaws

It may seem contrary, but creating a design that actually plays up a photo's flaws by imitating them helps make the imperfections work on a page. When the design mimics the look of the photo, the flaws suddenly make sense on a page. They help enhance a layout rather than distract from it.

Keep in mind that it was at least 85 degrees outside at 9am (or so it seemed) and Fletcher dehydrates like a prune after any physical activity··· So what happened next was naturally just supposed to happen, (ehem··· work with me here) As Fletcher ran with his cup full of water in the foot race, I noticed his cup being raised to his lips and giant gulps of that cool liquid dripping down his face, Hey, I suppose if you can't find a water fountain, make due with what you've got···GENIUS~ Fun Day May 2007

Despite the blurry photos, I had to tell this story of my son helping himself to the water he was carrying for a footrace game at school. The blur actually adds to the story, conveying a sense of action and frenzy, which I carried into my design. I incorporated splashes of paint and high-energy colors to provide a haphazard feel. The waves of red continue the idea of motion that matches the blur.

Supplies: Cardstock; patterned paper (CherryArte); letter stickers (Scenic Route); brads (Making Memories); Misc: Arial font, mesh, paint

THRILL
Of the
HUNT

Madison and I discovered that shopping together is incredibly thrilling when we find the perfect thing. We also enjoy the Mother/daughter bonding.   Madison's birthday shopping tradition 2007

My daughter and I have begun an annual tradition of taking a shopping trip for her birthday. These photos were taken under a store's fluorescent lights, which, combined with her movement, caused them to turn out dark and blurry. The arrow and circle embellishments on this page create a sense of movement that takes the emphasis off the blurry photos and creates an eye-catching layout.

Supplies: Cardstock; patterned paper (BasicGrey, Creative Imaginations); letters (Heidi Swapp, Making Memories); chipboard accent and sticker accents (Fiskars); rub-ons (Luxe)

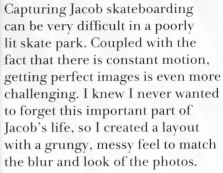

Capturing Jacob skateboarding can be very difficult in a poorly lit skate park. Coupled with the fact that there is constant motion, getting perfect images is even more challenging. I knew I never wanted to forget this important part of Jacob's life, so I created a layout with a grungy, messy feel to match the blur and look of the photos.

Supplies: Patterned paper, transparency (Hambly); letter stickers (Karen Foster); decorative tape (7gypsies); rub-ons (Making Memories); Misc: acrylic paint

How do you work with lots of clashing colors? Follow my lead. Here you can see a photo of my son at his birthday party at the skate park. I used a messy, random design to complement the mix of different colors and play up the look of the grungy park.

Supplies: Cardstock; patterned paper, rub-on accents (BasicGrey); letter stickers (American Crafts, Mustard Moon); Misc: Trashed font, mesh

The start of: **Christmas Morning**

Location: **Living Room**   Date: **12-25-06**

If happens so fast!
We go from a nice,
peaceful morning looking
at a beautiful tree packed
full of gifts for the kids
to a living room covered
in sheets of wrapping
paper and empty boxes
of toys.
The kids' eyes are glazed
over and their senses
are on overload. Where
to start. What to play with
first.
Ah - Merry
Christmas!

morning MAYHEM!

How many of us can relate to Kimber's thoughts about how quickly Christmas morning goes from beauty to mayhem? Her photos capture that frenzied feeling perfectly, and I love how she continued that theme with her design. The unstructured look of the letters and the background lines mimic the chaos in the photos. And the ripped blocks of paper bring out the theme of the page.

Artwork by *Kimber McGray*

Supplies: Patterned paper (Fontwerks); letter stickers (American Crafts): chipboard letters and accents (American Crafts, Fancy Pants); Misc: ink

Try Other Tricks

Using color and movement and embracing the flaws aren't the only ways to use design to make sour photos work on a layout. Here are some other great tricks to make some sweet pages.

some of the best fun happens when it's not planned...like a freak snowstorm, an unexpected day off school, an old sled, a bucket to dump snow on each other, and of course a high tolerance for the cold.

spontaneous

f
u
n

this ended up being one of the best days ever for abby and aaron...they stayed out all afternoon and wore each other out. and nobody made them play together.
I love it when that happens.
february '07

The white snow tricked Janet's camera into overexposing this photo of her children sledding, making any indication of snow disappear. Since the rest of the photo turned out great, Janet simply incorporated the overexposure into the layout's design as the background. The contrast between the white and the colors makes the photo pop, and the white background provides a clean base for this simple yet fun page.

Artwork by *Janet Ohlson*

Supplies: Digital Christmas brush by Anna Aspnes (Designer Digitals): letters by Katie Pertiet (Designer Digitals); Misc: Addict font

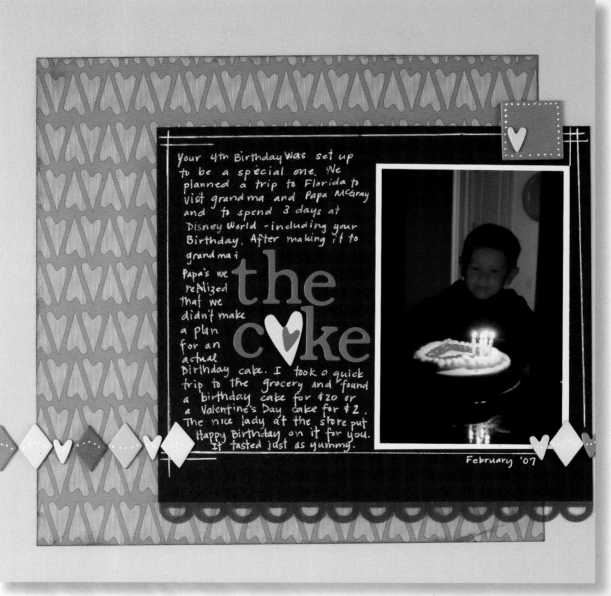

Your 4th Birthday Was set up to be a special one. We planned a trip to Florida to visit grandma and Papa McGray and to spend 3 days at Disney World - including your Birthday. After making it to grandma i Papa's we reAlized that we didn't make a plan for an actual Birthday cake. I took a quick trip to the grocery and found a birthday cake for $20 or a Valentine's Day cake for $2. The nice lady at the store put Happy Birthday on it for you. It tasted just as yummy.

the cAke

February '07

When Kimber showed me this page, I was intrigued by the hearts, which took the focus off an underexposed photo and placed it on her interesting design. I'm sure there aren't too many birthday photos that feature Valentine's Day embellishments, but the story she shares clearly warrants this design. Keep this trick in mind when you are creating a page with an interesting story: Going with the unconventional can turn a lemon into lemonade.

Artwork by *Kimber McGray*

Supplies: Cardstock; chipboard shapes, patterned paper, sticker accents (Heidi Grace)

3

Madison

Emily

Alvina

Hayley

Madison's 11th Birthday

Callie

Jailyn

Laura

Aubrey

Dance friends hung out with school friends... Swimming, jumping on the trampoline, creating fun crafts, sleeping over and having fun!

Take a Byte
Correcting photos with Photoshop Elements

The techniques in Adobe Photoshop Elements are fabulous recipes for making sweet layouts. With Photoshop Elements, the possibilities are amazing and nearly endless. Its capacity to eliminate your photo imperfections is almost beyond your imagination. Discoloration, background distraction, overexposure—they all disappear with just a few clicks of your mouse. In this chapter, I show you how Adobe Photoshop Elements can go a long way in turning your sour photos into the perfect pictures for your pages.

Introduction to Adobe Photoshop Elements

Photoshop has become one of the most popular image-editing software programs. I will admit that there is a learning curve to using it, and it did take me time to overcome some obstacles. However, the tricks and techniques in this chapter are pretty simple to learn and have saved my photos—and a ton of time—again and again.

When I first started working with Photoshop Elements, I learned through trial and error. After many frustrating rounds with this program, I found a great resource book, Scott Kelby's The Photoshop Elements 3 Book for Digital Photographers, and I began to teach myself new techniques. After reading through this chapter, if you find yourself interested in learning more, I recommend picking up one of Kelby's books for Photoshop Elements.

Before you begin following the instructions in the chapter, take note of a few things:

- Before you begin making changes to any photo, it's a good idea to save a copy of the original photo and work from the copy.

- I often refer to the Layers palette in this chapter. The Layers palette can be found on the right side of your screen (see right).

- I also refer to various tools in the toolbar. The toolbar can be found at the left side of your screen (see left). From top to bottom, the tools are: move, zoom, hand, eyedropper, marquee, lasso, magic wand, selection brush, type, crop, cookie cutter, straighten, red-rye removal, healing brush, clone stamp, eraser, brush, paint bucket, gradient, custom shape, blur and sponge. Clicking on the tool name provides a pop-up help screen explaining the tool.

- The instructions refer to Photoshop Elements 3, except where version 5 is specifically mentioned. Newer versions of Photoshop Elements will allow you to accomplish all of these specific techniques, but some of the steps may vary.

- The instructions are intended for PC users, but in most cases the steps are the same for Mac users.

Layers palette

Toolbar

Even if you don't have a computer or Photoshop, you can still make adjustments to digital photos using in-store photo kiosks. You'll find options such as an Enhancement button that will automatically adjust the color and lighting of your photo. Choosing the More Edits button will allow you to zoom and crop, remove red-eye, change to black and white or sepia tone, add text and borders, adjust the brightness/contrast and adjust the color (red/green/blue). These little machines pack a powerful editing punch!

Converting Photos to Black and White

Removing color can help disguise a number of photo flaws such as blurriness, colors that clash and poor lighting. Needless to say, learning how to quickly change a photo to black and white can be a very useful tool. After you learn how to remove the color from a photo, you can adjust the contrast and saturation to dramatize the photo if desired.

If you can believe it, this photo of my daughter and her teacher was at least the third try at capturing them together. All my efforts kept coming out blurry. So instead of torturing them with excessive attempts to get the photo right, I made the most of what I had and converted the photo to black and white. The result allowed me to focus on a vibrant design that matched the joy my daughter feels for her fifth-grade teacher.

Supplies: Cardstock; patterned paper (Doodlebug, KI Memories, Scenic Route); letter stickers (American Crafts); rub-on accents (BasicGrey); Misc: Times New Roman font, ribbon

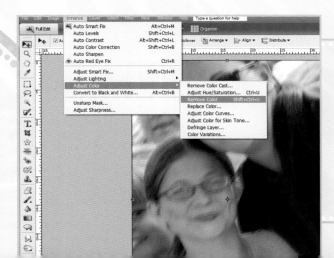

Remove Color is one of the quickest ways to make a photo black and white.

1 *Open your photo. Go to Enhance>Adjust Color>Remove Color to make the photo black and white.*

THIS PHOTO **ALMOST** DID not HAPPEN

Hot, sweaty and feeling unphotogenic ALMOST kept me from being willing to pose for this picture. What a huge lesson I've learned. I might have missed this incredible moment w/Madison at Scott's wedding. Summer 2004

This photo was taken on a very humid, sticky day at an outdoor wedding. I felt like I was melting and I really didn't want to have my picture taken, but afterward I was grateful to have this photo. The closeness between my daughter and me just shined through this picture, despite its flaws. So I made the photo black and white and gave it a glow using the Gaussian blur filter.

Supplies: Cardstock; patterned paper (American Crafts, Creative Imaginations); chipboard letters, letter stickers (Making Memories); chipboard accent (Everlasting Keepsakes); Misc: glitter

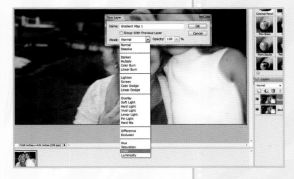

Although the Gradient Map option involves more steps than just Remove Color, it gives you a bit more control over the process. (You can also use this menu to make your photos different colors.)

1 *Duplicate your photo by going to Layer>Duplicate Layer. Then go to Layer>New Adjustment Layer>Gradient Map. A box will pop up. In the Mode field where it says Normal, select the drop-down menu and choose Color, then click OK.*

2 *The Gradient Map will open. Click on the long rectangle, and you will see the Gradient Editor. Click on the box that is half black, half white.*

➤ *To add a slight blur to your photo, in the Layers palette, click on the Background copy layer, then go to Filter>Blur>Gaussian Blur. Use the slider to adjust the pixels according to the amount of blur you'd like.*

Nic's layout illustrates another benefit to making a photo black and white. You just have to *oooh* and *ahhh* at this precious photo of Nic's daughter Abby. Making the change eliminated the color clash, allowing the precious moment, rather than all those distracting colors, to become the focus.

Artwork by *Nic Howard*

Supplies: Patterned paper (Autumn Leaves, BasicGrey, Jenni Bowlin, Scenic Route);

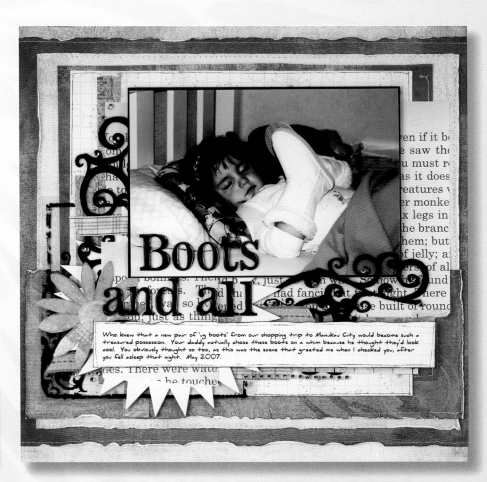

ALMOST 16!

I PERSONALLY BELIEVE IT'S THE TOUGHEST YEAR
OF YOUR LIFE. TOUGH BECAUSE YOU WILL FACE
TEMPTATIONS AND SOME WILL BE HARD TO RESIST.

IT CAN ALSO BE TOUGH TO STAY TRUE TO YOU!
I BELIEVE IN YOU...ALWAYS HAVE AND IF YOU
LIVE YOUR LIFE BELIEVING IN YOURSELF,

YOU WILL BE ABLE TO
SAY WITH PRIDE..

MY
...life
IS MY MESSAGE.

This photo of Jacob had a serious tone that I felt called for a black-and-white conversion. I also wanted to disguise the blemishes that often happen during the teenage years. The black-and-white photo conversion was the perfect choice to allow the handsome features of my son and his pensive attitude to come through.

Supplies: Digital patterned paper by Audrey Neal (Mosh Posh); frame by Katie Pertiet (Designer Digitals); brushes, paper by Anna Aspnes (Designer Digitals); embellishment by Tia Bennett (Two Peas in a Bucket); Misc: Last Font I'm Wasting on You font

The black-and-white conversion in Photoshop Elements 5 is one of the easiest options for removing color with control over the outcome.

1 *Open your photo and duplicate the layer (Layer>Duplicate Layer). Then go to Enhance>Convert to Black and White.*

2 *You will have the option of increasing or decreasing red, green and blue. You can also adjust the contrast to your preference. So simple!*

This was my second attempt at scrapping this photo. My son's nighttime sleeping habits are a source of comfort for me, and I wanted this page to reflect that. The first design—with bold colors to match the photos—didn't quite measure up to the feel I was hoping to convey. The second time around I made the photo black and white to neutralize the colors. That way, I could create a design that was soft and soothing.

Supplies: Cardstock; patterned paper (Scenic Route); letter stickers (Mustard Moon); brads (Making Memories); Misc: Bookman Old Style font, ribbon

Correcting Lighting, Color and Contrast

Photoshop Elements offers several options—from one-step fixes to those that allow more control over the results—that make amazing improvements to photos with flaws like underexposure and age.

I bet the sounds of disco fever are playing in your head when you look at this layout. The colors of my cute little dress and the tablecloth all give off a '70s vibe. Unfortunately, the original photograph has a retro orange cast to match. But no worries! Auto Smart Fix helped the image show its true colors. Then, I played up the vintage theme by incorporating them in my design and adding a bit of crochet.

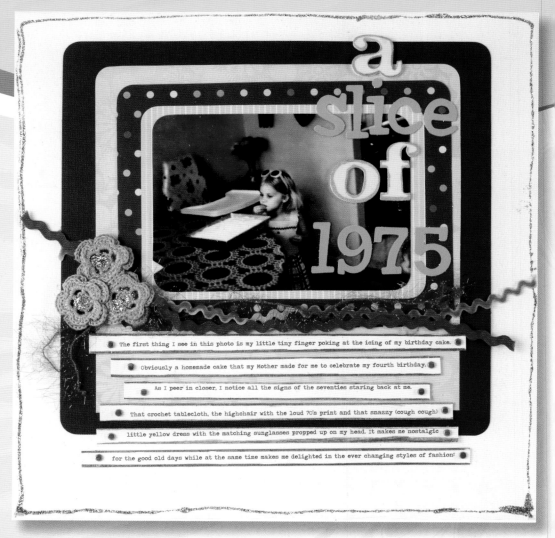

Supplies: Cardstock; patterned paper (Autumn Leaves, SEI); letter stickers (American Crafts); crochet flowers (Imaginisce); brads (Making Memories); Misc: Typedenski font, glitter, gold leafing pen

With one click, Auto Smart Fix adjusts the lighting and color of an image. There isn't any control with this option, but it allows you to fix photos quickly.

1 *Open the photo in Photoshop. Go to Enhance>Auto Smart Fix. How easy is that?*

This picture has special meaning because it was a rare occasion when I got in the picture with one of the kids. I was usually the one taking the pictures. To have this picture of the two of us together and to have us both looking good in the picture is a rare moment that I will always cherish.

This is my absolute favorite birthday picture of Sherry and me I love the way we both look and the closeness of the two of us while Sherry cuts her cake. She was dressed in her new birthday outfit with her sunglasses on her head and her beads around her neck. This picture was taken in Rapid City, South Dakota. This picture was taken on June 15, 1976

In my MOM'S words

Not only is this one of my favorite photos, it is also one of my mother's favorites. But the color of the actual photo was faded and discolored, which took away from the beauty of the moment. Bringing the color back to its original form allowed me to create a layout that does the image justice.

Supplies: Digital vintage paper, overlay, tag by Rhonna Farrer (Two Peas in a Bucket); Misc: paper, typewriting font

I used to spend time with this group of ladies when I first started scrapbooking. We had lost touch over the years, but ran into each other a little while ago. It was so neat to see that one of my old pals had started her own line of scrapbook products (seen on this page) and that everyone was still scrapbooking. This photo was underexposed, but image editing went a long way toward improving this picture. The new and improved photo became the perfect starting point about a page reflecting on those happy times spent with scrapbooking friends.

Supplies: Cardstock; journaling card, patterned paper, sticker accents (Dude Designs); letter stickers (Making Memories)

Auto Levels is the perfect choice for a one-click fix to the contrast of an image.

1 *Open the photo and go to Enhance> Auto Levels. Simple as that. The photo is lightened, and it took only one step!*

This photo has some pretty harsh shadows, but I wanted to do my best to save it so I would always remember our first year living near the beach. Using a quick image editing trick allowed me to brighten up and even out the shadows so I could focus on the warmth and love of the moment without the distracting poor exposure.

Supplies: Cardstock; patterned paper (7gypsies, American Crafts); letter stickers (American Crafts); chipboard letters (Heidi Swapp); chipboard accents (Everlasting Keepsakes); rub-ons (Fancy Pants); clip (7gypsies); Misc: conchos, ink, ribbon

The Screen option in Photoshop quickly lightens an underexposed photo, but it takes a few more steps than Auto Levels. Those extra steps allow you more control over the end result.

1 *Open the photo and duplicate the layer (Layer>Duplicate Layer). In the Layers palette, open up the drop-down menu (where it currently says Normal) and select Screen. Adjust the opacity to the desired lightness. A little adjustment with the contrast gave me the results I desired.*

Lugging around the equipment required to take photos in full sunlight can be inconvenient when you are at an amusement park. But without it, I found myself taking photos with harsh shadows and glare that couldn't be avoided. I lightened these photos using Photoshop, but they still needed more help, so I used a colorful design to make the photos work. The white background provides the contrast needed to brighten the look of the photos. Plus, the visual triangle in orange draws the eye around the page.

Supplies: Cardstock; acrylic letters (Heidi Swapp); chipboard shapes (Bazzill); Misc: paint

If you want to have precise control over the adjustment of a photo's brightness and contrast, try the Adjust Lighting option.

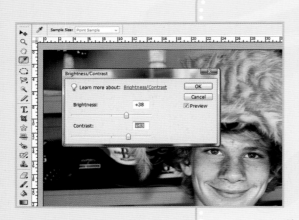

1 *Open the photo and duplicate the layer (Layer>Duplicate Layer). Then go to Enhance>Adjust Lighting>Brightness/Contrast. When the box pops open, move the Brightness slider until the photo lightens the desired amount. Adjust the Contrast to increase the color and saturation in the photo, as needed. The amount you adjust will vary based on the amount of underexposure in your photo.*

When my husband and son got together, their playing made for a great photo moment, but the lighting in my living room isn't always the best. I simply adjusted the brightness and contrast to brighten the washed-out color.

Supplies: Cardstock; patterned paper (Daisy D's, Imagination Project, Junkitz); chipboard letters (Li'l Davis, Making Memories); chipboard accents (Heidi Swapp, Urban Lily); ribbon (7gypsies, Heidi Swapp); brads (Making Memories); Misc: Type A font, corrugated cardboard, ink

This layout required the use of both Photoshop and a little ingenuity to help make the image work. In the photo, Linda's son is underexposed. The obvious solution was to brighten the photo. But when she did, the background became too light. So Linda used two copies of the photo: She brightened one copy, cut out her son and layered it over the other copy with adhesive foam.

Artwork by *Linda Harrison*

Supplies: Cardstock; chipboard letters and accent, patterned paper (Creative Imaginations); die-cut letters (Xyron)

When I snapped these photos in my poorly lit living room, I purposely turned off my flash in order to get a warm tone. Of course, that resulted in these dark photos. So Photoshop helped me brighten the photos and increase the contrast. Then I created a layout that would convey the warmth of the moment.

Supplies: Patterned paper (Crate Paper, Melissa Frances); chipboard letters (American Crafts, Heidi Swapp); brads (Making Memories); die-cut shapes (Crate Paper); Misc: corrugated cardboard, wire mesh

This photo has special meaning to me since my grandfather recently passed away. As I looked at this image before scrapping it, I realized the washed-out photo would do well with a little tweaking of the contrast and color. The new version has sharpness for clarity and more color saturation, helping to enhance the story the photo tells.

Supplies: Cardstock; letter stickers (Scenic Route); brads (Making Memories); stamp (7gypsies); Misc: ink

Merge Photos

The Photomerge option is one of my favorite ways to merge scans of a two-page layout. This feature is also great for merging photos. However, you should note that this feature is not meant to combine any two images, but to create one continuous panoramic photo from two separate but almost identical photos (for example, photos capturing a city skyline).

Recently I discovered Photomerge would work well for two photos that I took of a group shot at my daughter's birthday party. I couldn't back up far enough to get all the girls in the frame, but I ended up with two photos that contained most of the girls in each. I simply merged the two photos and ended up with all the girls in one photo for a nearly perfect birthday shot.

Supplies: Cardstock; patterned paper (Crate Paper); chipboard flowers and bookplate (Everlasting Keepsakes); brads, tags (Making Memories); Misc: glitter

1 Open both photos. Go to File>New> Photomerge Panorama. A box will pop up to verify the images that you want to merge. Click OK.

Eliminate Red-Eye

Removing redness in the eyes is a simple process that is quick to complete in Photoshop. With just one easy step, you make a total lemon supersweet.

As you can see in the before photo, my children's red eyes are glowing—not the most attractive look. I quickly corrected that flaw to salvage this photo, since red-eye is hard to simply disguise. But an assortment of other photo imperfections remained. I decided to use those flaws as the starting point of my page theme.

Supplies: Cardstock; patterned paper (BasicGrey); chipboard letters (Rusty Pickle); Misc: Papyrus font, bookplate, ink, ribbon, transparency

1 Open the photo that needs correcting and select the red-eye remover tool located in the toolbar on the left side of the screen. (It looks like an eye.) Move the cursor over each eye and click. Voilà! The redness is removed.

➤ *Note: The key to a natural appearance is to adjust the darken amount (in the toolbar at the top of the screen) to around 7 to 10 percent. It darkens the pupils but still allows light to shine through the eyes.*

YOU ARE SPECIAL COUSIN

Chloe, Billy and Sophie have so much fun playing together. Billy is their very special cousin! 10-04

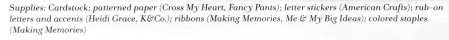

Looking at this sweet moment that Suzy captured of her daughters and their cousin, you can just feel the love between them. These photos were almost perfect in every way except for those glowing red eyes. Using the red-eye correction, she was able to quickly improve them and let the warmth of the moment shine through instead.

Artwork by *Suzy Plantamura*

Supplies: Cardstock; patterned paper (Cross My Heart, Fancy Pants); letter stickers (American Crafts); rub-on letters and accents (Heidi Grace, K&Co.); ribbons (Making Memories, Me & My Big Ideas); colored staples (Making Memories)

Here's another example of how a small fix can make a big impact and allow you to save a photo. Kimber has the cutest kids, and the red-eye correction helped make this photo of Andrew and Laura even cuter.

Artwork by *Kimber McGray*

Supplies: Cardstock; patterned paper (Around the Block, Heidi Grace, Making Memories); letter stickers (American Crafts); sticker accents (Making Memories); chipboard accents (Fancy Pants); Misc: floss

tra·di·tions
(tr dsh 'n) n.

1 - the passing down of culture from generation to generation

2 - family ritual repeated regardless of popularity

At Christmas time we travel to visit family the week before the big day. At Papa Gary and Grandma Karen's house - the christmas showcase is the mantel with all 20 stockings hung from tiny nails. Everyone has a stocking with their name on it in glitter. Everyone tries to find theirs to make sure Santa has a place to park their goodies. But, it's like pulling teeth to get a photo of the kids in front of them. 12/06

THE photo

Bill   Andrew   Laura   Kimber

Remove Distractions

Poles and plants growing out of people's heads seem to be common in photos. And anyone who has a family member with glasses knows the problem of eyeglass glare. The clone tool in Photoshop is a great way to eliminate such small distractions. The process can take some time and effort, but with practice and patience use you can clone your way to practically perfect photos.

Anyone that meets Madison becomes instantly aware of the perfectionist in her. She sets very high standards for herself and for those around her. As I stand back and watch her with her friends, I realize that she emerges as the leader in most situations. People can sense that she has confidence and knows what she likes. She simply does not like when things do not go as she planned. I often wonder how someone like me gave birth to someone like her. It is not to say that I don't want things to be done right. On the contrary, I just don't set myself up for the perfectionism that I see in her. I try to be realistic and understand that things may not always go exactly as planned. As I begin to wonder where she got this trait, I suddenly realize that even though I do not require that everything go exactly as I see it in my head, I DO expect a lot from Madison. I have set some pretty high standards for her to follow. Many of which I know she can achieve because I know my daughter. Many of those standards are set high because she is the only daughter and I have high hopes for her. There are standards for her that may be considered double standards to some because she is a girl. Things like expecting her to help around the house more (although it's really only because she does a much better job than her brothers) and getting straight A's (but this is because she has a proven track record of being brilliant with her studies). I realize that she is mostly her Father's personality when it comes to her standards but the apple didn't fall far from the tree when it comes to my own expectations. At least where my daughter is concerned. I will always expect great things from her and I don't anticipate that she will disappoint. I only write this to her as a caution to try to keep things as realistic as possible and keep things in check often. As I give that advice to her, I will also take note of it for myself. I promise to not have unrealistic expectations and to always encourage in any situation. Hopefully we will balance each other's standards. I will always love you no matter what!

Madison & Sherry

2007

Madison and Sherry

Photos of my daughter and me together often inspire me to share words of wisdom. When I use meaningful journaling within my pages, I hope that my daughter will relate to my messages in times of doubt throughout her life. I am very grateful that I was able to salvage this photo, using the clone tool to remove my daughter's glass glare, because it has turned out to be one of my favorite photos of the two of us.

Supplies: Patterned paper (Crate Paper, Fancy Pants, Scenic Route); chipboard accents (Everlasting Keepsakes); metal accents (7gypsies, Making Memories); Misc: ribbon, title letters

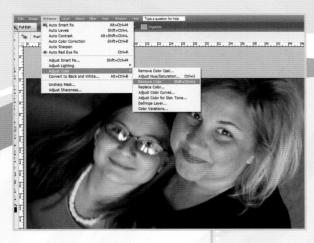

1 First, open your photo and duplicate the layer (Layer>Duplicate Layer). Remove the color by going to Enhance>Adjust Color>Remove Color.

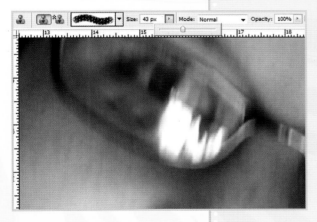

2 Use the zoom tool at the left of the screen to zoom in close to the area you want to clone. Then locate the clone tool in the toolbar at the left side of your screen (it looks like a stamp).

3 A menu will pop up at the top of your screen. Select Normal as the mode, and choose the brush size that will work best for the size of your imperfection. Choose a small size (here, I used 29 pt) to start, and then increase or decrease the size based on your needs. Leave the opacity at 100 percent.

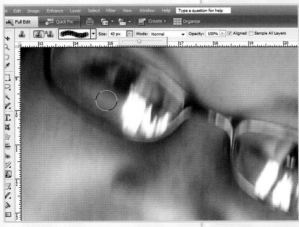

4 Place your cursor over the area of the eye that doesn't have glare; click <alt> then click your mouse to select the area to clone. Then place your cursor over the area with the glare you want to remove and click your mouse. A cross will appear to show you what area you are cloning. Continue to click over the area with the glare until it is removed. Repeat these steps to remove glare from the other eye. To finish, adjust the brightness and contrast as desired.

new beginning Jacob's Adventure

As he begins his third year in high school, I sense that he has started to realize that it's time to take school and life a little more seriously than he has in the past. There is something different about his attitude and perspective. From the Honors classes he has chosen to take to the enthusiasm he has begun showing for the subjects, it is obvious that he is starting to grow up and take a closer look at his responsibilities. He is also driving to school with his sister as his passenger and is expected to be extra cautious. While we've had a few bumps in the road of life (with Jacob you always got to expect the unexpected), I expect that we will have a new beginning to a better year.

A+ 2007

back to the pencils, back to the books, back to the teacher's dirty looks.

Jacob has had many struggles in school, but it's not because he's not bright enough to handle the workload. It is more a case of lacking motivation. I had some pretty high hopes for him at the start of his junior year of high school, knowing there were many new things he was about to experience. This page documents the new beginning he was about to embark upon. I cloned out the tree branch to make sure my son, and not the distraction, remained the focus of the page.

Supplies: Cardstock; patterned paper, rub-ons, sticker accents (BasicGrey); letter stickers (American Crafts, Making Memories); Misc: Cambria font, transparency

Here, I use the clone tool to remove a tree branch in the background.

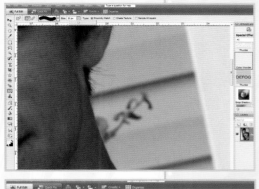

1 *Open your photo and duplicate the layer (Layer>Duplicate Layer). Use the zoom tool to zoom in on the area you want to delete from the photo (in this case, the tree branch). Select the clone tool at the right of the screen, choose Normal as the mode, and select your brush size in the menu at the top of the screen. The smaller the size, the more precise cloning you can create. Leave the opacity at 100 percent.*

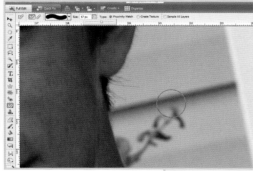

2 *Place your cursor over the area you want to clone; click <alt> then click your mouse to select the area to clone. Then place your cursor over the area with the object you want to remove and click your mouse. A cross will appear to show you what area you are cloning. Continue to click over the area with the object until it is removed.*

school's out

It didn't take too long for the boys to grab their boards and beg to be taken to the beach once that school bell rang for the last time.

June '06

Fletcher & Alec

Here's another example of cloning out distraction. Keep in mind that it took me a lot of time and patience to remove the larger subjects from this photo. But the result is a fabulous photo with the focus on my son and his best friend, the inspiration for this page showcasing the ritual of heading to the beach once school was out of session.

Supplies: Digital patterned papers and overlay by Veronica Ponce (Two Peas in a Bucket)

Add Selective Color

Selective coloring is great when you want to highlight the subjects of your photo with color while minimizing the background by making it black and white. This technique improves photos with busy background colors or colors that clash.

At the time Thomas was gaga over

this local singer (Mr. Knickknack) who played guitar

and he mimicked and imitated him constantly.

His first "guitar" was that purple racket my daughter's wearing.

'05 6 31

He was given the ukulele when she was born...
I grabbed the camera b/c she grabbed his "purple guitar"
and started imitating Thomas.

GUITAR hero

My friend Deborah had this fantastic photo of her son and daughter with a cute story to go with it. The background was so full of colors and distractions that it was hard to focus on the sweet children. When she shared it with me and asked me to see what I could do with it, I felt that selective coloring would be the perfect solution. Deborah's children loved their guitars and when I removed the background, those guitars took center stage.

*Supplies: Cardstock; patterned paper (Sassafras Lass);
letter stickers (American Crafts, Chatterbox);
brads (Making Memories); sticker accents (Daisy D's)*

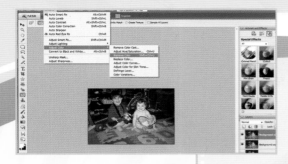

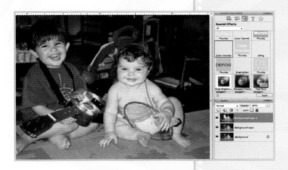

1 Open your photo and duplicate the layer (Layer>Duplicate Layer). Make sure the new layer is selected and duplicate that layer (Layer>Duplicate Layer). When you look at your Layers palette, you will have three layers with your photo (the background and two copies).

2 Select the top layer (Background Copy 2) in the Layers palette and make that layer black and white. Go to Enhance>Color>Remove Color.

3 Make sure the black-and-white layer is selected. Choose the eraser tool from the toolbar on the left side of the screen. In the menu at the top of the screen, select the size brush you want; choose a small size for more detailed erasing. Then hold down your mouse button and erase the areas in which you want color. When you're finished, go to Layers>Flatten Image.

This photo is overexposed and in it the boys are wearing colors that clash with the subject (the soda bottle). Both of these photo flaws made it difficult to determine the best approach for this page. Using the selective color technique allowed the bottle to become the focus and also made it easier to select complementary colors for the layout.

Supplies: Cardstock; patterned paper (CherryArte, Luxe); letter stickers (American Crafts); rub-on letters (Luxe); brads (Making Memories); chipboard accents (Everlasting Keepsakes); Misc: mesh

Turn a Photo Transparent

In this chapter we've seen that you can lighten a photo in a number of ways. Here is one more technique to add to your repertoire. Turning a photo transparent can mask the underexposed image and create an interesting look.

Jacob and I rarely take photos together, so I was happy to have these, which we took ourselves using the camera's timer. Even though we cut off our heads in the original photo, I still liked the expressions we captured. Making this photo transparent and placing it on the edges of the page is a great way to mask its imperfection.

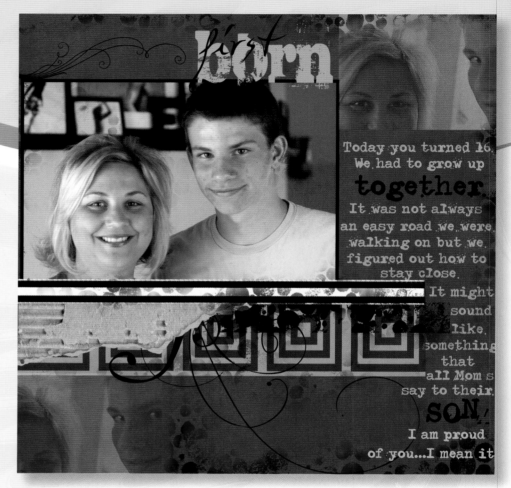

Supplies: Digital brushes by Anna Aspnes (Designer Digitals); corrugated element (Designer Digitals); Misc: Trashed font

1 Open the photo and resize it to the dimensions you want to use for your page. Do this by going to Image>Resize and then typing in the height and width. Open a new file (File>New>Blank File) and fill in the Preset as custom, the width and height as 8.5" × 11" (22cm × 28cm), Resolution as 300 pixels/inch, RGB color and a white background.

2 Click on the move tool (the arrow) in the toolbar at the left of your screen. Click on your photo and drag it into the blank file. In the Layers palette at the right side of your screen, select Layer 1, then click on the Opacity slider and move it until you achieve the desired transparency.

Apply Artistic Filters

Like their name suggests, artistic filters add an artistic touch to your photos. Use these techniques to improve any number of imperfections. I usually play with several filter options to see which one best achieves the look I want for my photo.

Suzy had her son take this photo of her and her husband. She loved how he captured the love between them but wasn't thrilled with how out of focus the image was. She decided to try using an artistic filter, and the results are inspiring. She followed up with a layout that enhances the romantic island theme.

Supplies: Cardstock; patterned paper (Rusty Pickle); chipboard letters (Fancy Pants); chipboard accents (Heidi Grace); brads, rub-ons (Creative Imaginations); ribbon (Li'l Davis); staples (Making Memories)

Artwork by *Suzy Plantamura*

1   *Open the photo. Go to Filter>Brush Strokes> Crosshatch. Adjust the three sliders (Stroke Length, Sharpness and Strength) until you reach your desired results. Hit OK when you're finished.*

Give Photos a Vintage Look

Blending various effects in the Layers palette can create a dreamy look for your photo. This is a fantastic way to disguise blur as well as other photo flaws.

This photo records one of those rare moments when all three of my children were in a warm embrace, loving each other. I am so glad that we finally got rid of that couch my children are sitting on. It always clashed with everyone that sat on it! Using this dreamy technique darkened the background just enough so the couch was no longer visible, and I was free to create this soft, beautiful page about the bonds of family.

Supplies: Die-cut title, patterned paper (My Mind's Eye); flowers (Prima); buttons (Autumn Leaves); chipboard accent (Everlasting Keepsakes); stamps (Hero Arts); transparency (Hambly); Misc: ink, ribbon

1 Open the photo and crop it as desired. To do so, click on the crop tool in the toolbar at the left of the screen. Drag your mouse over your photo until the area you select covers the area you want to keep.

2 Duplicate your photo (Layer>Duplicate Layer). At the top of the Layers palette, click on the drop-down menu that says Normal and change it to Soft Light.

3 Click the eyeball icon next to your background layer in the Layers palette to hide it. Duplicate the new layer (Layer>Duplicate Layer). You should now have three copies of your photo in the Layers palette. Click on the middle layer and go to Enhance>Adjust Color>Remove Color to make it black and white. Duplicate that middle layer twice (go to Layer>Duplicate Layer two times). You should now have a top color layer, three middle black-and-white layers and a bottom hidden background layer.

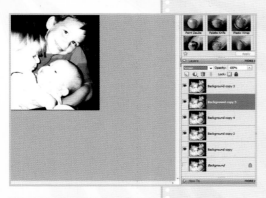

4 In the Layers palette, click on the second layer from the top. In the drop-down menu, change Soft Light to Screen. With this second layer still selected, go to Filter>Blur>Gaussian Blur. Set the pixels to 10.

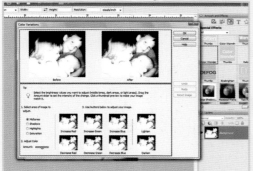

5 With this particular photo, I wanted to darken the photo image so I took it one step further. Go to Enhance>Adjust Color>Color Variations. Select Midtones and Darken. When you're finished, go to Layer>Flatten Image.

Highlight Part of a Photo

Digitally highlighting part of a photo is a great way to focus on one area of a picture while keeping the background visible. This look can be achieved using a transparency or vellum paper, but using Photoshop to create the look is less messy and requires only one tool!

every one loves a PARADE

Caleb's boy scout troop took part in the Memorial Day Parade. The route started at Lourdes College and ended at Veterans' Memorial field. It was a long route but Caleb was lucky. He spent a good portion of the parade riding in a yellow convertible and passing out candy to the crowds. Memorial Day Parade May 2007

It is clear that this photo of my friend's son during a Memorial Day parade is filled with many other people that distract from her son. My friend wanted to see if I could come up with a unique approach that would highlight her son's participation. I chose this technique, which makes him the focus while still allowing the reader to see that he was riding in a yellow Corvette.

Supplies: Patterned paper (Cosmo Cricket, Rusty Pickle); die-cut letters (Cosmo Cricket); chipboard accents (Everlasting Keepsakes, Li'l Davis); rub-ons (Li'l Davis); Misc: Old Typewriter font, twine

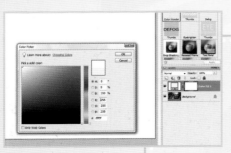

1 *Open your photo. Go to Layer>New Fill Layer>Solid Color. Click OK to create a new layer entitled Color Fill 1. Select the color for your overlay (I used white) and click OK.*

2 *Go to the Layers palette and move the Opacity slider to about 50 percent. Make sure the color fill layer is selected.*

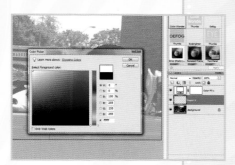

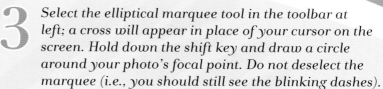

3 Select the elliptical marquee tool in the toolbar at left; a cross will appear in place of your cursor on the screen. Hold down the shift key and draw a circle around your photo's focal point. Do not deselect the marquee (i.e., you should still see the blinking dashes).

4 Go to Edit>Fill Selection. Under Contents, select Black and click OK. Make sure your marquee circle is still selected (the circle should be blinking). Then go to Layer>New>Layer and hit OK. Set your foreground color as white by going to the boxes at the bottom right of the toolbar and double clicking on the top box. Select white as your color.

5 Go to Edit>Stroke (Outline) Selection. Type a wide width (such as 20 pixels) and click OK. Now you can deselect the circle. Flatten the layers (Layer>Flatten Image) to finish.

The problem with Janet's photo was not a distracting background, but a subject that just faded away. Janet used the highlighting technique in order to draw attention to the subject. It not only highlights the subject, but adds depth and dimension to the design and helps the words become an important part of the page.

Supplies: Digital paper by Mindy Terasawa (Digi Chick); swirl accent by Anna Aspnes (Designer Digitals); Misc: Geo Sans Light and Steelfish Outline fonts

Artwork by *Janet Ohlson*

4

DANCE with joy

It makes me smile to see how you
can so easily amuse yourself.
It doesn't matter where we are or
what we're doing, you're happy.

You just seem to overflow with excitement,
and it's like you enter your own little world

This day, we were waiting for the Blooming
festival parade to begin.

While everyone else was trying to find a good spot to sit
and feeling a little cranky from the heat, you were content
to dance happily along the edge of the street.
I hope you never lose that joy.

Jonathon
May '06

Make Lemonade
Gallery of ideas for using sour photos

This gallery features many different layouts that effectively illustrate the methods for making lemonade out of your photos that I've discussed throughout the book. In it, you'll see many photo flaws as well as examples of combined approaches to designing around those imperfections. Whether you're looking for more hints on how to work with problematic photos or just want some delicious design ideas, turn the page for lots of layout inspiration!

knock!

boo boo boo boo boo boo boo boo boo boo boo boo

happy halloween ● happy halloween ● happy halloween

trick
or
treat

Halloween
2006

Just as it started to get dark, we headed out trick-or-treating. Andrew RAN to every house that had a porch light on. He KNOCKED and waited patiently. "TRICK OR TREAT!" he yelled once the door was open. Misson completed!

Kimber had a blurry, poorly lit photo taken from a distance without zoom working against her when she created this layout. A simple change to black and white reduced many of the photo flaws, but what makes this layout really stand out is the eye-catching design with blocks of bold color. Kimber's style is fun and modern with a twist of something unique. The details enhance this photo and make this page sweet.

Artwork by *Kimber McGray*

Supplies: Cardstock; patterned paper, sticker accents (Heidi Grace); letter stickers (American Crafts)

imitation is the sincerest form of *flattery*

Ella really enjoys going to football games and watching Abby cheer for the Cowboys. Lately she's learned enough of the cheers that she can do them along with the team. I don't know who likes it more, Ella or Abby, but it's pretty cute either way. Go Cowboys!
october '07

These photos remind me of my own childhood with my younger sister. She followed my every move. I love that Janet's daughters have that same sweet relationship. What Janet found when she began to scrap these photos were distracting colors and people in the background. Combining two techniques—clever cropping and removing the color—gave her the perfect foundation for a fantastic layout.

Artwork by *Janet Ohlson*

Supplies: Digital papers by Katie Pertiet (Designer Digitals); Misc: Porcelain and Times New Roman fonts

The sour elements in these photos include overexposure, distractions and a person who isn't part of the story. I had snapped this photo of the bus so quickly that I didn't notice it wasn't my kids' bus. I also missed capturing the "real" bus when it arrived. As a result, I had only this bus photo. I cropped the bus, and changed it to black and white to help downplay the washed-out image. I also used the clone tool to get rid of the car and soda machine in the other photos. I topped it all off with an eye-catching design that incorporates splashes of red to draw the eye around the page.

Supplies: Digital embellishments, papers and title letters by Tia Bennett (Two Peas in a Bucket); Misc: 2Peas Think Small font

SUNSET BEACH

I first discovered Sunset Beach when I was twenty-two.
I thought it was the most beautiful beach I had ever seen and I
kept a postcard picture of it on my desk for years hoping to
some day be able to return. We found Sunset Beach on our
vacation to Oahu and twenty-two years later my dream came true.

Aug. 2007

Suzy captured a special moment between her children in this photo. What she noticed, however, was not the moment, but the mass of open space above her children. But, the sky looked so beautiful Suzy didn't want to crop it out. Using the expanse of sky to hold the title helps the eye focus on the kids without losing the beauty of the scenery. Suzy used additional photos of scenery to create the title letters—a great way to crop flawed photos.

Artwork by *Suzy Plantamura*

Supplies: Patterned paper (Rusty Pickle); letters (Maya Road); rub-ons (Creative Imaginations)

enlarge size
mask distractions

This photo needed zoom manipulation and overexposure adjustment. After I enlarged the photo and cropped out the excess, I used Photoshop to pump up the color. I added a bright color scheme and used embellishments to mask distractions. Finally, I added a catchy title to tie in my journaling.

Supplies: Cardstock; patterned paper (BasicGrey, Scenic Route, SEI); letter stickers (American Crafts, KI Memories); brads (Making Memories)

This visit to Six Flags in Chicago was the 1st time Jason had been to an amusement Park! A grown man going to a place of fun for the first time was almost as much fun to see as it was to see Jacob (8) Madison (3) & Fletcher (1)

Sept '99

for your amusement

apply filter
give a vintage look

If I look past the blur in this photo, I can see it captures the essence of being near the ocean. I found a filter in Photoshop that gave this image a dreamy quality to match the feeling I wanted for the layout. I also combined the Gaussian blur and vintage look techniques, and added a lot of journaling to make that the focus.

TIDE blue

When I was a little girl my family and I used to go on vacation to the beach. Even then, I knew that there was a certain pull of the ocean that drew me into its spell. I longed to spend hours at the edge of the ocean, drinking in it's beauty. Many years later, I still feel the pull of the ocean and I discovered that my daughter is also drawn to it's majestic powers. She is growing up near the ocean so she has the ability to experience this pull as much as she wants. This brings me great joy to see the ocean through her eyes. Moving to the coast has been one of the best things that we've done. It has awakened my senses and allowed my children to experience the love of the ocean. A love that we will share the rest of our lives. photo 2006

Supplies: Cardstock; patterned paper (BasicGrey, Creative Imaginations, Doodlebug); rub-ons (BasicGrey); Misc: rhinestones, transparency

The shots on this layout were taken at different times. That fact, along with their age, made for faded photos mismatched in size and color. But that didn't stop me from making a great page! I used Photoshop's Auto Levels to restore the color on one photo. I removed the color on another photo and designed the page so that each black-and-white photo bookends the color photo. Plus, the swirly design and bright colors draw the eye across the page. In the end, I was able to create a special layout about an old high school friend who still holds an important place in my heart.

Supplies: Cardstock; patterned paper (7gypsies); letter stickers (American Crafts, Karen Foster); rub-ons (BasicGrey); transparencies (Creative Imaginations, Hambly)

I had a blast following my children around the park with my camera. With all the shooting, I suspect anyone observing my behavior that day would have thought these children were famous. I just couldn't get enough of the bright colors and their incredible smiles. What I also got was a big dose of dark and blurry photos. I lightened many of them in Photoshop and decided to embrace the blur as part of the story.

Supplies: Cardstock; letter stickers (Doodlebug); dingbat shapes (Two Peas in a Bucket); Misc: Angelia font, ribbon, transparency

Quite possibly one of your favorite birthday gifts this year...this awesome Buzz Lightyear jersey and a matching football from Aunt Bean and Uncle Keith. You were so excited when you opened it I thought you might explode! You were so proud showing off your new jersey and then quickly ran outside to play with the new Buzz ball. They got you the perfect gift and you were so happy to be just like Buzz!

just like
★ BUZZ

Here, Kelly lightened the main photo using the Photoshop screen technique. It did a beautiful job of taking that photo from overexposed to just right. While this is a fabulous trick that helps make this page terrific, the real design elements I found intriguing were the black-and-white photos. The creative cropping and reduced size not only minimize the distracting background, but add a sense of movement to the page. All of Kelly's design tricks work together to keep the focus on the subject rather than the photo flaws.

Artwork by *Kelly Noel*

Supplies: Cardstock; patterned paper (Arctic Frog); chipboard letters (Heidi Swapp); brads, chipboard accents, letter stickers (American Crafts)

109

Not only is my son's body cut off in the photo at right, the image is overexposed. All in all, the point of the photo gets a little lost. First, I adjusted the lighting and contrast. Then, to draw out the story as well as minimize the photo flaws, I placed emphasis on the journaling in my layout. Using black journaling strips draws attention to the words, and the curvy lines created by their placement lead the eye down the page to the title—and away from the photos.

Supplies: Cardstock; letter stickers, patterned paper (American Crafts); chipboard letters (Heidi Swapp); ribbon (Making Memories); brads (Fiskars)

My name is Janet, and I am a **pitcher's mom**

It's that time of year again...time to sit nervously in the stands, instructed by Abby not to say ONE SINGLE WORD to her while she's pitching... time to bite my nails and hold my breath with each pitch...time to cheer when she throws a good one... time to groan (silently) when she misses...time to breathe a sigh of relief when the inning is finally over. Yes, it's time to be a pitcher's mom again. **Give me strength!** May 2007

Janet did a great job of making the photo on this page pop. She used bright colors to create energy on the page and to highlight the great hues in the photo. And using the open space for journaling helps maximize the photo's potential.

Artwork by *Janet Ohlson*

Supplies: Digital paper by Anna Aspnes (Designer Digitals); overlays, stamp and staples by Katie Pertiet (Designer Digitals); Misc: Georgia and Impact fonts

our B boy

Once upon a time...

was a little bit on the chunky side
It's hard to believe when you see
him today

Was our only
child... but
soon we discovered
one wasn't
enough and we
added two more

1991

was so
happy and
easy to be
around... &
he still is

We love you
Jacob 3mos

Using decorative transparencies to cover the clutter in the background was the perfect trick to enhance this photo of my son and my husband. The original photo benefited from a black-and-white conversion, and a decorative embellishment brought the photo to center stage.

Supplies: Cardstock; die-cut title, patterned paper, transparency (My Mind's Eye)

The KiwiScraps event in April 07 was awesome.

Some of the best times were had in the bar at the events centre.

Inbetween classes and during downtimes it was always guaranteed someone would be there.

It was time to sit and eat a meal, grab a drink or just sit and enjoy the company.

Fun city, good times, great new friends. Enough said.

Artwork by *Nic Howard*

Just because some of a photo's subjects have their backs to the camera doesn't mean it can't work on a page. In fact, when Nic shared this layout with me, I didn't notice at all that the photo was poorly framed. The enlarged image made me feel like I was sitting in the same room with these ladies, eavesdropping on their conversation. Plus, converting this photo to black and white gives it an "arty" photojournalistic quality, perfect for imperfect framing.

Supplies: Cardstock; patterned paper (Scenic Route); brads, chipboard letters, flowers (Queen & Co.); sticker accents (7gypsies); rub-ons (Hambly); ribbon (Fancy Pants); transparency by Rhonna Farrer (Two Peas in a Bucket); Misc: Screenwriters Nightmare font

The couch you see in the original photo (at right) is a piece of our family history, but it took away from the focus in these photos of my son. The story of his obsession with Batman is primary to this layout, so I decided to use the overlapping technique to keep from completely cropping out the couch. This layout also incorporates a lot of journaling, placing the focus on the story behind the photos.

Supplies: Cardstock; patterned paper (Fontwerks); letters (American Crafts): transparency (Hambly); Misc: Hall of Heroes font

I was thrilled that I got to spend some in-person time with these three friends. We met at a trade show and went to lunch. The lighting in the restaurant was dim, and I didn't have my camera set correctly, but luckily I found that changing this photo to black and white solved the issues of poor lighting and blur. Designing with high-impact colors and wavy lines creates movement and energy that draw attention to the design.

Supplies: Cardstock; patterned paper (CherryArte, KI Memories, Scenic Route); letters (traced from Everlasting Keepsakes product); ribbon (7gypsies); Misc: paint, transparency

DANCE
with
joy

It makes me smile to see how you
can so easily amuse yourself.
It doesn't matter where we are or
what we're doing, you're happy.
You just seem to overflow with excitement,
and it's like you enter your own little world

This day, we were waiting for the Blooming
festival parade to begin.

While everyone else was trying to find a good spot to sit
and feeling a little cranky from the heat, you were content
to dance happily along the edge of the street.
I hope you never lose that joy.

Jonathon
May '06

My friend Crystal shared this photo of her son dancing down the street during a town parade. Some simple cropping was all it took to remove the distractions, but I was still left with a lot of open space to work with. So I took the empty space as the perfect place for my journaling, using the masking technique to hide the background. I love this technique because it gives a photo context while preventing the openness from dominating the page.

Supplies: Patterned paper (Crate Paper, Rusty Pickle); tags (Making Memories); paper frills (Doodlebug); Misc: ribbon

I'm not sure how this photo of my daughter didn't come out blurry. After all, I had to have been laughing hysterically while Madison was giving me this "if looks could kill" stare. Even though this photo is perfectly clear, it suffers a multitude of other problems, including a cluttered background, red eyes and overexposure. So, I decided to focus on the story and use journaling and bright colors to create a sweet layout.

Supplies: Cardstock; patterned paper (CherryArte, Doodlebug, Urban Lily); chipboard letters (Heidi Swapp); brads (Making Memories); Misc: ribbon

I discovered these photos on my camera. I love that

Jacob captured this moment between M & F

I might have missed this

check this out
moment

I have a hands-off policy when it comes to my camera. But on this particular day I was very grateful that Jacob broke it. Otherwise, I would have missed this special moment. Because Jacob's not familiar with the settings on my camera though, really dark photos were the result. I lightened them a bit, but even the best image editing couldn't clear them up. Sometimes, the best "fix" for poorly lit photos is just to accept them as they are. I felt there was a charm to the imperfections, as if I were spying on the game, so I grouped the photos together in a series to showcase the action in several steps.

Supplies: Digital flourish, paper, staple by Leora Sanford (Little Dreamer); grunge overlays by Katie Pertiet (Designer Digitals); Misc: A Charming, Chunk Type and Type-Ra fonts

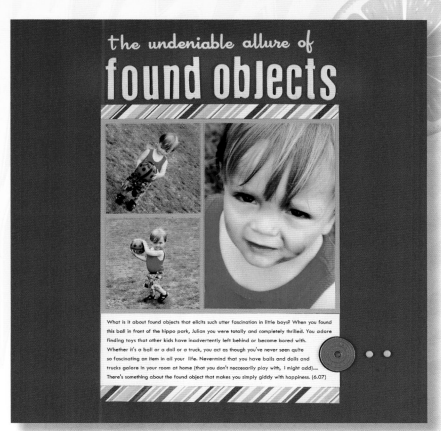

the undeniable allure of
found objects

What is it about found objects that elicits such utter fascination in little boys? When you found this ball in front of the hippo park, Julian you were totally and completely thrilled. You adore finding toys that other kids have inadvertently left behind or become bored with. Whether it's a ball or a doll or a truck, you act as though you've never seen quite so fascinating an item in all your life. Nevermind that you have balls and dolls and trucks galore in your room at home (that you don't necessarily play with, I might add).... There's something about the found object that makes you simply giddy with happiness. (6.07)

Supplies: Cardstock; brads, patterned paper (We R Memory Keepers); chipboard letters (Heidi Swapp); rub-on letters (American Crafts); Misc: TwCen MT font

Here, Hillary used image editing and clever cropping to create the cutest of pages. The original photos were a bit dark, so Hillary used Photoshop to lighten and brighten them. In one original photo, her son's hand is blurry, drawing the eye to it. This distraction takes away from the best part of the photo. But Hillary was able to crop out the blurry hand so the focus remains on her son's adorable face, making for a precious page.

Artwork by *Hillary Heidelberg*

crop out flaws

create movement

How lucky to get a group shot with the entire ship showing! I cropped this photo to reduce the distractions. I also placed a large red circle in the background to frame the page and draw the eye in a circle. And try this trick: Pair a larger, better photo with a bad photo to diminish the flaws.

This was the first cruise we ever took.

The purpose was to celebrate our 25th wedding Anniversary.

The cruise was from February 1, 1997 through February 8, 1997.

The ports that we visited on this cruise were

San Juan, St. Thomas, Guadeloupe, Granada, Caracas, and Aruba.

Our good friends Matt and Jane Hoffman went on this cruise.

This photo of us was taken as we were getting off the ship at Aruba.

With great friends like them, our vacation was...

SMOOTH
Sailing

Supplies: Cardstock; patterned paper (Dream Street, My Mind's Eye); letter stickers (Making Memories, Scenic Route); ribbon (Heidi Swapp); brads (Making Memories); Misc: Old Typewriter font

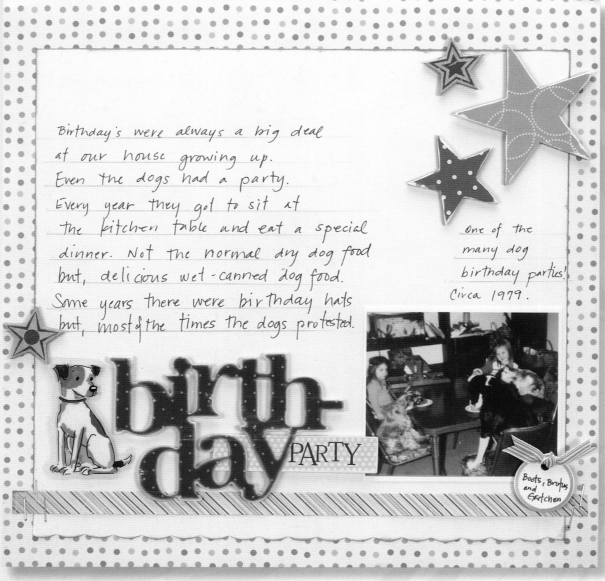

Birthday's were always a big deal at our house growing up. Even the dogs had a party. Every year they got to sit at the kitchen table and eat a special dinner. Not the normal dry dog food but, delicious wet-canned dog food. Some years there were birthday hats but, most of the times the dogs protested.

One of the many dog birthday parties! Circa 1979.

birthday PARTY

Boots, Brutus and Gretchen

Kimber used both color and movement to enhance this vintage photo. The bright colors and light page background balance out the darkness of the photo as well as pull out the photo's brighter colors (green and yellow). Plus, the movement created by the visual triangle of embellishments—the single star, circle tag and grouping of stars—draws the eye around the page, right past the flaws and to all the fun.

Artwork by *Kimber McGray*

Supplies: Cardstock; patterned paper (Cosmo Cricket, Daisy D's, Li'l Davis, Scenic Route); chipboard title, sticker accents (Me & My Big Ideas); ribbon (May Arts); Misc: decorative scissors, ink, staples, tag

I gasped after I took this photo. After a closer look, I discovered that stray hair that had wandered in front of of your face.

At first I was disappointed that I didn't get a perfect shot but then I realized a valuable lesson that I should share with you. The importance of cherishing what on the surface may not be what you were expecting but as you look closer, discover the treasure of being....

Slightly imperfect

The imperfection in this photo actually became the topic of this page. Can you see the stray hair that fell in front of Madison's face? It became the starting point for the theme of the layout. I felt that this layout was a perfect way to wrap up this book because it embraces the fact that sour photos can be turned into sweet layouts if you just embrace the possibilities.

Supplies: Digital labels and papers by Rhonna Farrer (Two Peas in a Bucket); Misc: Papyrus and Sidewalk fonts

contributors

Linda Harrison has a love for design, color, photography and storytelling—all of which unite to form her passion for scrapbooking and papercrafting. Linda has been creating in some form or another since she was a child. In 2005, she took her creating to another level when she began doing freelance work in the craft industry. She has since designed for a variety of manufacturers and has had her work published in several publications. In addition to being the author of *Starting Points* (published by Memory Makers Books in 2008), Linda was inducted into the 2007 Creating Keepsakes Hall of Fame and was featured as a Scrapbook Trends Trendsetter for 2006. When she's not creating, Linda enjoys filling her days with fun family times with her husband and son, reading and enjoying the beaches in her hometown of Sarasota, Florida.

Hillary Heidelberg has been scrapbooking for more than five years, and it has truly become an obsession. She loves creating sharp, clean designs that capture the everyday moments in her life. She lives in the heart of Manhattan with her two young boys, Luca and Julian, and her wonderful husband, Michael. She runs online classes at nycscraps.com and loves reading fiction, running and playing with her boys. She is also the author of Memory Makers Books' *Scrap Simple*.

Nic Howard lives in New Zealand with her husband and three children and has been scrapbooking for nine years. She confesses to having scraps of paper littering the floor and small handmade paper items in every nook and cranny of her house. In 2004, Nic won a place in the Memory Makers Masters competition. Her work appears frequently in both Memory Makers books and magazine. She juggles this work alongside freelancing for other publications, manufacturers and distributors in the scrapbooking industry. Her largest and most fulfilling accomplishment to date is the release of her book *That's Life: Finding Scrapbook Inspiration in the Everyday*, published by Memory Makers Books.

► *Kimber McGray*, always a crafter of some kind, started scrapbooking three years ago and has never looked back. "Obsessed" would be a mild way of describing her love of papercrafting. Over the past two years, Kimber's work has been published in *Memory Makers, Creating Keepsakes, BHG Scrapbooks Etc., Scrapbook Trends,* and *Scrapbook and Cards Today* magazines, as well as featured in different idea books. Her work has also appeared in major ad campaigns for We R Memory Keepers. Kimber was named a Creating Keepsakes Hall of Fame 2007 winner. She lives in Carmel, Indiana, with her husband of eight years, Bill, and two children, Andrew and Laura.

► *Kelly Noel* started scrapbooking in college, and it quickly became an obsession after her first son was born in 2004. She likes to scrapbook late at night when the rest of her family is asleep, and she finds the hobby to be a great creative outlet. She really enjoys and is almost never without her camera. Kelly lives in Florida with her husband and their two young sons.

► *Janet Ohlson* is a native Texan who now lives in the Chicago suburbs. She is a mom to four active kids and wife to David, and she works as a choir director and pianist. She looks at scrapbooking as creative therapy, and she enjoys both paper and digital scrapbooking. She has been published many times in magazines and idea books, and she was named an Honorable Mention in the 2007 Creating Keepsakes Hall of Fame contest.

► *Suzy Plantamura* has been creating scrapbooks of one sort or another since she was in grade school. She has always loved making art and collecting photos and memorabilia, so when she became a stay-at-home mom eight years ago, scrapbooking became her passion. Suzy designs projects and pages for Maya Road, Love, Elsie and MAMBI. She was named a Memory Makers Master in 2006 and has been a contributor to many of the Memory Makers books and magazines. She lives in Southern California with her three children and husband and loves to spend time at the beach.

Source Guide

The following companies manufacture products featured in this book. Please check your local retailers to find these materials, or go to a company's Web site for the latest product. In addition, we have made every attempt to properly credit the items mentioned in this book. We apologize to any company that we have listed incorrectly, and we would appreciate hearing from you. Companies with an asterisk (*) after their name generously donated product toward the creation of the artwork in this book. Special thanks to Prism Papers for generously donating cardstock toward the creation of artwork in this book.

7gypsies*
(877) 749-7797
www.sevengypsies.com

A2Z Essentials
(419) 663-2869
www.geta2z.com

Adobe Systems Incorporated
(800) 833-6687
www.adobe.com

Adornit/Carolee's Creations
(435) 563-1100
www.adornit.com

American Crafts*
(801) 226-0747
www.americancrafts.com

Arctic Frog
www.arcticfrog.com

Around The Block
(801) 593-1946
www.aroundtheblockproducts.com

Autumn Leaves
(800) 588-6707
www.autumnleaves.com

BasicGrey*
(801) 544-1116
www.basicgrey.com

Bazzill Basics Paper
(480) 558-8557
www.bazzillbasics.com

BoBunny Press*
(801) 771-4010
www.bobunny.com

Chatterbox, Inc.
(208) 461-5077
www.chatterboxinc.com

CherryArte*
(212) 465-3495
www.cherryarte.com

Cosmo Cricket*
(800) 852-8810
www.cosmocricket.com

Crate Paper*
(801) 798-8996
www.cratepaper.com

Creative Imaginations*
(800) 942-6487
www.cigift.com

Cross-My-Heart-Cards, Inc.
(888) 689-8808
www.crossmyheart.com

Dafont
www.dafont.com

Daisy D's Paper Company
(888) 601-8955
www.daisydspaper.com

Deluxe Designs - *no longer in business*

Designer Digitals
www.designerdigitals.com

Die Cuts With A View
(801) 224-6766
www.diecutswithaview.com

Digi Chick, The
www.thedigichick.com

Doodlebug Design Inc.
(877) 800-9190
www.doodlebug.ws

Dream Street Papers*
(480) 275-9736
www.dreamstreetpapers.com

Dude Designs*
www.dudedesignsonline.com

EK Success, Ltd.
www.eksuccess.com

Everlasting Keepsakes*
(816) 896-7037
www.everlastingkeepsakes.com

Fancy Pants Designs, LLC*
(801) 779-3212
www.fancypantsdesigns.com

Fiskars, Inc.*
(866) 348-5661
www.fiskars.com

Fontwerks*
(604) 942-3105
www.fontwerks.com

Hambly Screenprints*
(800) 707-0977
www.hamblyscreenprints.com

Heidi Grace Designs, Inc.
(866) 347-5277
www.heidigrace.com

Heidi Swapp/Advantus Corporation*
(904) 482-0092
www.heidiswapp.com

Hero Arts Rubber Stamps, Inc.
(800) 822-4376
www.heroarts.com

Holly McCaig Designs
www.hollymccaigdesigns.com

Imagination Project, Inc.
(888) 477-6532
www.imaginationproject.com

Imaginisce
(801) 908-8111
www.imaginisce.com

Jenni Bowlin
www.jennibowlin.com

Junkitz
(732) 792-1108
www.junkitz.com

K&Company
(888) 244-2083
www.kandcompany.com

Karen Foster Design
(801) 451-9779
www.karenfosterdesign.com

KI Memories
(972) 243-5595
www.kimemories.com

Li'l Davis Designs
(480) 223-0080
www.lildavisdesigns.com

Little Dreamer Designs
www.littledreamerdesigns.com

Luxe Designs*
(972) 573-2120
www.luxedesigns.com

Making Memories*
(801) 294-0430
www.makingmemories.com

Martha Stewart Crafts
www.marthastewartcrafts.com

May Arts
(800) 442-3950
www.mayarts.com

Maya Road, LLC
(877) 427-7764
www.mayaroad.com

Me & My Big Ideas
(949) 583-2065
www.meandmybigideas.com

Melissa Frances/Heart & Home, Inc.*
(888) 616-6166
www.melissafrances.com

Mosh Posh
www.mosh-posh.com

Mustard Moon
(763) 493-5157
www.mustardmoon.com

My Mind's Eye, Inc.*
(800) 665-5116
www.mymindseye.com

One Heart...One Mind, LLC
(888) 414-3690

Pressed Petals
(801) 224-6766
www.pressedpetals.com

Prima Marketing, Inc.
(909) 627-5532
www.primamarketinginc.com

Prism Papers*
(866) 902-1002
www.prismpapers.com

Queen & Co.
(858) 613-7858
www.queenandcompany.com

Ranger Industries, Inc.
(800) 244-2211
www.rangerink.com

Rouge de Garance
www.rougedegarance.com

Rusty Pickle*
(801) 746-1045
www.rustypickle.com

Sassafras Lass
(801) 269-1331
www.sassafraslass.com

Scenic Route Paper Co.*
(801) 542-8071
www.scenicroutepaper.com

SEI, Inc.
(800) 333-3279
www.shopsei.com

Stampin' Up!
(800) 782-6787
www.stampinup.com

Sugar Giggles
www.sugargiggles.com

Sweetwater
(800) 359-3094
www.sweetwaterscrapbook.com

Tinkering Ink*
(877) 727-2784
www.tinkeringink.com

Two Peas in a Bucket
(888) 896-7327
www.twopeasinabucket.com

Urban Lily*
www.urbanlily.com

We R Memory Keepers, Inc.
(801) 539-5000
www.weronthenet.com

Wordsworth
(877) 280-0934
www.wordsworthstamps.com

Xyron
(800) 793-3523
www.xyron.com

Index

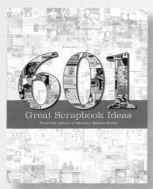

601 Great Scrapbook Ideas
Brimming with inspiration and ideas, you'll discover one amazing page after another in this big book of layouts.
ISBN-13: 978-1-59963-017-5
ISBN-10: 1-59963-017-6
paperback
272 pages
Z1640

Expressions
Taking extraordinary photos of ordinary life is easy with the help of Donna Smylie and Allison Tyler Jones. Learn the basics of lighting and composition, view a gallery of striking photos paired with inspiring subject-specific ideas, and get insider tips for snapping timeless images of your own touching moments and special occasions.
ISBN-13: 978-1-58180-909-1
ISBN-10: 1-58180-909-3
paperback
128 pages
Z0526

See what's coming up from Memory Makers Books by checking out our blog:

www.mycraftivity.com/ scrapbooking_papercrafts/blog/

Focal Point
Discover unique and stunning ways to showcase your favorite photos with these fresh and fabulous photo altering and transfer techniques.
ISBN-13: 978-1-892127-96-9
ISBN-10: 1-892127-96-2
paperback
128 pages
Z0530

Paper + Pixels
Discover the world of hybrid scrapbooking! Try 40 simple lessons that give you the how-to for using digital techniques that are as fun as using scissors and glue. Includes a bonus CD with 10 exclusive scrapbook kits.
ISBN-13: 978-1-892127-93-8
ISBN-10: 1-892127-93-8
paperback
128 pages
Z0350

These and other fine Memory Makers Books are available at your local scrapbook retailer, bookstore or from online suppliers, or visit our Web site at *www.memorymakersmagazine.com* or *www.mycraftivity.com.*